A MILLION DOLLARS IN
CHANGE

HOW TO **ENGAGE** YOUR EMPLOYEES,

————— **ATTRACT** TOP TALENT, —————

AND **MAKE** THE WORLD A BETTER PLACE

ALESSANDRA CAVALLUZZI

WISE Ink
CREATIVE ★ PUBLISHING

ISBN 13: 978-1-63489-103-5
eISBN: 978-1-63489-104-2
Library of Congress Catalog Number: 2017959203
Printed in the United States of America
First Printing: 2017

21 20 19 18 17   5 4 3 2 1

Cover design by Nupoor Gordon

Wise Ink Creative Publishing
837 Glenwood Ave.
Minneapolis, MN 55405
www.wiseinkpub.com

To order, visit www.itascabooks.com or call 1-800-901-3480.
Reseller discounts available.

TABLE OF CONTENTS

Great acts are made up of small deeds.

—Lao Tzu

PREFACE

I've always considered myself a people person. I'm not shy by any means. As a child growing up in New York, I dreamed of being a famous actress. I would put on performances for my family on our stoop, singing and dancing, pretending to be on a Broadway stage. I loved living in a big city. When I was a teenager, my family decamped to Long Island, or as we city kids referred to it, "the country." Truth be told, it wasn't farms and cows; but having grown up around taxis, alleyways, and subways, I was definitely in culture shock. Those first days of high school were interesting. People would approach me not so much because I was the new girl, but because I was from "the City," which was almost, as I understood it, like being from a foreign country.

Over the years, I continued to dream of performing. I took drama classes and acted in school plays. I loved it: the adrenaline rush of opening night; the excitement backstage as you waited for your cue to step out into the spotlight. Looking back, I realize now what I loved the most was how the performances made the audience feel, more so than how they made me feel. My performances offered the audience an escape from the mundane and made them smile. For three acts, they could forget their day-to-day lives and the challenges that came with them. If they were struggling, they could relate to a character I was portraying and feel a little less alone. I saw performing as a way to do good, to give something back to the people who came to see me. And that made me feel great.

Since my theater days, I've played quite a few roles. I've worked for law firms, insurance companies, financial institutions, and equipment distributors. I've held positions in human resources, marketing, and project management, to name a few. I've managed large teams and given countless presentations. Through it all, one thing has remained a constant: the desire to give back, the need to make a difference. In fact, that desire was so strong in me that I helped my company develop a program to help the communities around us that's now in its twelfth year.

If you've picked up this book, chances are you have a passion for serving others, but you're not quite sure how to get started. Perhaps you've been researching current issues in your community and want to help solve them, but the prospect of actually diving in and taking action feels huge and overwhelming. Maybe you're already involved as a volunteer and want to inspire your peers to join you. Maybe you're an HR leader looking for a way to breathe life into your company's culture. Or perhaps you're a CEO who wants to prepare your company to step up to the challenge of changing the world. Sound like you? Then you've found the right book; or, perhaps, the right book has found you. *A Million Dollars in Change* will show you how to energize your employees, build a better company, and improve your community by creating a workplace giving program.

LEARNING THE LINGO

In the course of this book, we'll talk about *charitable giving* (also known as corporate philanthropy) and *corporate social responsi-*

bility (CSR). Now, I've seen them used interchangeably, and I've seen them described as completely different animals. The truth is, they are not exclusive of each other, but they are a little bit different. *Charitable giving* encompasses donations or grants made to a nonprofit organization. If you've ever made a donation to fund cancer research, for instance, this is a form of charitable giving.

Corporate social responsibility, on the other hand, *can* include philanthropy, but these programs have other functions, too. A company might design a CSR program, for instance, to improve the well-being of its employees, the environment, and the community around it. A company with a CSR program might partner with a nonprofit to keep at-risk teens in school by enrolling them in training and educational programs. Maybe a company gives young adults in underserved communities internships to learn marketable skills. Perhaps employees volunteer their time and talent to help a local nonprofit. It's not uncommon for a company with a CSR program to reduce its carbon footprint by making changes like installing solar panels or energy efficient lighting, or doing away with Styrofoam in its packaging. All of these are examples of CSR.

The important thing to remember is that your program doesn't need to be one or the other to be successful. Which term you use to describe your program will depend on whether you decide to go strictly with philanthropy, create a full CSR plan, or maybe even develop a hybrid—donations plus action. At my company, we use the term "charitable giving," even though we incorporated volunteerism and some of the other aspects of CSR. Charitable giving most accurately reflected where our focus was, and so that felt right to us. Also, as I was developing our program, I knew that we would not be able to implement a full-blown CSR program right out of the gate because that type of program would require a much bigger investment, and that would have made it harder to get the initial funding we needed to get off the ground. So we started with a charitable giving program that we could scale up in the future, leaving us plenty of runway for growth.

SEPARATING FACT FROM FICTION . . . AND FEAR

Many business leaders and HR professionals have told me over the years that they want to launch a charitable giving or CSR program in their company, but they feel intimidated and don't know where to begin. I've been approached by people who have told me that they want to embed the values of service and community into their organization to create a "giving culture," but they fear they will come up against resistance, either from employees or management. Others have worried they are "just one voice" and don't think that they'll be taken seriously.

And let's face it, there are quite a few myths surrounding corporate giving and CSR programs that keep otherwise motivated and capable people from taking action. Maybe you've heard this one: "CSR is a 'nice to have' but not a 'need to have,' because it's not tied to core execution." Maybe you've heard, "Why bother with charitable giving? There's no return on investment (ROI)." But the one I hear most often? "Starting a charitable giving program takes money—lots of it. We just don't have the budget for that."

In the following chapters, I'll debunk these myths and show you, once and for all, that developing a charitable giving program is as good for your company as it is for your community—and it doesn't require nearly as much in start-up funds as you might think. In fact, many aspects of these programs can be done at little or no cost to your company.

As for your doubts and fears? I had them, too. But the good news is that creating a workplace charitable giving program isn't as hard as you think. The even better news is that I'm going to tell you how to do it. And the best news of all? There are things you can do right out of the gate that don't require a big investment and will make you look like a rock star.

MY STORY

Twelve years ago, before I had the green light from my higher-ups, support from my colleagues, or a dime of funding, all I had was a vision, and a pretty broad one at that. I wanted to take my company's charitable giving program to the next level, and I wanted this bigger and better program to make our employees proud, attract the best people to our company, and help others in the process. I wanted a program that reflected our awesome company culture and enabled us to take it outside our walls and into the community. I wanted to combine charitable giving with opportunities for our employees to be hands-on agents of change. I knew that volunteering was a perfect way to do this, and I was eager to introduce this concept to my company. I had ideas for working with nonprofits to help solve issues that our communities face each and every day: homelessness, veteran unemployment, illiteracy, and poverty. I knew what I wanted to do. I just had to figure out how to do it.

I began searching online for information on how to develop and implement a corporate giving program, but all I could find was data on why it was critical for companies to adopt giving or

CSR as part of their strategy. I came across plenty of great articles and reports that talked about the benefits of having a CSR program and the consequences of not adopting a CSR strategy as part of a business strategy. I read all about "social investing" and "social enterprise." But for someone starting from square one, I found this information to be too complex and completely overwhelming. I realized soon enough that I was pretty much on my own. I thought, "I could just forget this idea, or, I could take a chance and try to do this myself." In the end I decided on the latter, and I set out to develop a plan to build a workplace giving program for my company. What started as a journey to create a program led to the creation of a department and a new career path for me.

Over the years, I've been told by nonprofits and community organizations alike that the program in place at my company is unique not so much because of its structure, but because of how we engage our employees. One of the things that makes our program different from most is that it's not micromanaged by our main office. Although the program is run out of our corporate headquarters, it involves employees at all levels of the company in all of our locations. We have dedicated employee volunteers who serve on what we call "community relations teams" that help us plan and execute various programs and events throughout the year in partnership with a wide variety of nonprofits. Time and again I am told that our philosophy toward community service, our culture of giving, and our hands-on approach to support is refreshing.

YOUR STORY STARTS HERE

No matter where you are or how big your company is, *A Mil-*

lion Dollars in Change will help you develop a program that's right for your business and your community. It doesn't matter what language you speak or which continent you're on. The program you design will be successful because at its very core will be your desire to help others and make the world a better place. You might not realize it now, but that desire is universal. In the course of our work together, you'll learn how to customize a program to fit your company's culture, its mission, and most importantly its budget. What you'll create won't just be a corporate giving program, but a company culture of giving.

CHAPTER 1

MYTHS, MISCONCEPTIONS, AND MISUNDERSTANDINGS

Plenty of people want to do good in their companies and communities, and lots of those people have fantastic ideas. But putting ideas into action can be intimidating if you don't know where to start, and it can be especially discouraging to be told it can't be done, it shouldn't be done, or that it *has* to be done a certain way or what's the point. In the preface, we discussed a few oft-repeated myths around workplace giving programs and CSR. I've heard them used as excuses, sure, but plenty of people actually buy into them, which is a shame, to say the least. Imagine how many HR and business leaders out there are letting a little thing like a myth stop them from catalyzing change. Maybe you're one of them!

So let's get a few things straight, shall we?

Myth #1: CSR is a "nice to have," but it's not a "need to have" because it doesn't impact a company's core strategy execution.

Reality: In fact, CSR is an essential driver of employee engagement. According to a study conducted by America's Charities, sixty-eight percent of employers said that their employees expect them to provide:

- an effective workplace giving program
- the ability to volunteer during work hours
- opportunities to engage skills-based volunteering
- matching gifts for employee contributions to nonprofits

When you provide your employees with opportunities to participate in company-sponsored fundraisers, volunteerism, and charity events, you're helping to drive engagement. You may have heard engagement defined as how "happy" or "satisfied" employees are. In fact, there is a distinct difference between *satisfied* employees and *engaged* employees. Satisfied employees like their jobs and are happy to come to work. They do what is required of them, and they perform their job functions well. Engaged employees go a step further. They bring a passion and a higher level of commitment to their job. They have a sense of purpose, strive to achieve more, and are fully invested in their company's success. Engaged employees are your biggest asset, and through their participation in your program, they will serve as champions of not only your culture, but also your company's image and brand.

Workplace giving and CSR programs, when incorporated into a company's strategy and embedded into its culture, help to strengthen an employee's emotional commitment and increase the emotional investment employees make in their company. In addition, if you take it one step further and give employees a voice, inviting them to offer ideas and feedback about your program on a regular basis, you are also empowering them. Empowerment is a great motivator and driver of engagement. Engagement and empowerment contribute to higher performance, which in turn leads to higher productivity. It should go without saying that employee performance and productivity levels have a direct impact on successful core strategy execution.

Myth #2: There's no tangible return on investment (ROI) associated with workplace giving and/or CSR programs.

Reality: Corporate giving plays a critical role in how your company is perceived by all of your stakeholders, which without a doubt impacts your ROI. For one thing, your employees are your company's biggest ambassadors. Through volunteerism they help raise the visibility of your brand and also strengthen your reputation as a good corporate citizen. Your employees are your corporate culture in action. No marketing campaign on the planet can compare with that kind of PR. Consider, too, that your customers expect you to be active in supporting your community. Edelman's goodpurpose study found that forty-four percent of consumers believe companies should allow employees time to volunteer. According to Edelman, "Corporate volunteer programs not only boost employee morale—they also can be great reputation boosters."

A culture of giving enhances your company's image, and image is everything. For starters, the image your company projects is important to your employees. It can impact whether they stay or go. A company's image can impact whether candidates apply for a job with you or pass in favor of another company, and whether potential customers choose to do business with you or someone they feel is more socially invested.

If your company, like many others, is struggling to engage your millennial workforce and/or appeal to millennial consumers, consider this: A report sponsored by the Case Foundation with research from Achieve states that millennials expect corporations and employers to be committed to doing good. According to the report, millennials collectively spend $300 billion annually on consumer discretionary goods. In 2013, a whopping eighty-seven percent of them donated to a charity. Given that this group will make up fifty percent of the workforce by 2020, it's even more important that companies weave giving into their business strategies. While employee retention is important, attracting new talent to your company is just as crucial. The Case Foundation's Millennial Impact Report notes that "if a company wants to recruit and hire a talented, civic-minded millennial, company-sponsored cause work is an important selling point." Millennials between the ages of twenty-five and thirty were more likely to accept a position if they heard about cause work in the interview. Indeed, recruiters at my company have reported that candidates have mentioned our company's community involvement and charitable giving during the interview process.

Today, corporate philanthropy is about cultivating a relationship with nonprofits that goes beyond the donation grant and involves identifying a need in the community and working together to help meet it. Writing a check to a charity but also showing up with a team of employee volunteers early on a Saturday morning shows commitment to building a lasting partnership with a nonprofit. Giving employees the opportunity to be a part of company volunteer teams specifically dedicated to helping you implement your program engages and empowers them. It also allows you to tap existing resources to get the job done, creating a win-win.

So to recap: charitable giving and CSR contribute to retention, recruitment, employee engagement, enhanced company reputation, and increased brand visibility. I'd say that's a pretty good return on investment!

Myth #3: You need to invest a lot of money in a workplace giving program to do it right.

Reality: Perhaps the biggest myth I've heard about starting a workplace giving program, and the one that's at the heart of why I wrote this book, is that you have to make a significant dollar investment to launch a program. You will be happy to know that not only is this *not* true, but you can actually launch your program with little to no investment and still make an impact in your community. How do I know? Because that's exactly what I did.

Many events, such as clothing and food drives, cost your company nothing and still benefit nonprofits and the people they serve. Organizing a volunteer effort is also a no- or low-cost activity. Starting your program off with these types of events has other benefits as well. It gives you an opportunity to gauge employee interest, and in doing so allows you to gather data to build a case for future funding and program expansion. Understand that there is no such thing as "not good enough" when it comes to giving. Doing *something* trumps doing nothing any day. (More on how we launched our program on a shoestring budget and still made a meaningful impact in chapter 7, "Charter Your Course.")

Now that we've dispelled the myths, it's time to start planning your reality: how you'll help your company create a million dollars' worth of change (without spending a million)!

Key takeaways from this chapter:

- There's no "wrong way" to give
- Satisfied employees are not engaged employees

- Millennials expect corporations and employers to do good
- Doing something trumps doing nothing every time

CASE STUDY

Values and Purpose-Driven Giving: Wallick & Volk

In this chapter we talked about a new style of philanthropy that goes beyond the checkbook. This approach to giving focuses on identifying a need in the community and collaborating to help meet that need. It's about relationship building, a concept that Wallick & Volk understand well.

Wallick & Volk Mortgage in Phoenix, Arizona, was recognized by *Phoenix Business Journal* as one of the best places to work in Phoenix. They pride themselves on their values, which are:

- Operate with trust
- Act with good purpose
- Strive for excellence
- Conduct ourselves with integrity
- Encourage personal responsibility

These values resonate, especially given how hard this part of the country was hit by the foreclosure crisis and predatory lending in the mortgage industry. In addition to their values, the company is also known for their philanthropy. On its website, the firm has a link to GivingBack, a program that provides discounted home loans and other real estate services to community heroes (retired and active government employees; current and former members of the military; public and private school employees; medical workers; and emergency services personnel). Giving-Back is the only program of its kind in the United States. It was designed to target, screen, and maintain a strategic network of professionals and companies that provide quality assistance to community heroes at discounted prices not available to the general public.

The impact of this type of program can be measured by the number of loans given and how many homes are purchased. In addition, a program that works directly with individuals on a one-to-one basis helps establish the company as a true community partner via the relationships that are forged between the firm and the people it serves. The company also educates the community on the types of assistance they qualify for as a result of their profession or status as a first-time home buyer. Key to the success of Wallick & Volk's program is that the work they are doing in the community ties back directly to their business and their core values.

Is there a product or service your company sells that you can provide to a nonprofit? Can that product or service benefit members of your community? Are there certain groups within your community that have expressed a need for the service or product? If so, then a program like the one at Wallick & Volk might be perfect for your company.

CHAPTER 2

SCOUT IT OUT

I guess you could say that I was always drawn to charitable causes and helping others. I credit my mother and grandmother with my passion for community service, as they were always putting the needs of others before their own. My mother, Jane, has always been a very giving person. I remember many times as a child hearing her say that you should perform random acts of kindness and lend a hand to those who need it most. My grandmother, Angelina, was a very religious woman. A Roman Catholic by birth, she attended Sunday mass every week and would spend most of her days reciting the rosary. One of the fondest memories I have of my "Nonna" was when I found her reciting her prayers one day in her apartment. I asked her why she was always praying, because it seemed to me that she was never without her rosary beads. I remember joking with her that if she couldn't get into Heaven with all the praying she'd done over the years, then surely there was no hope for the rest of us. She replied, "I'm not praying for myself, I'm praying for our family." When I asked why, she said, "I know how busy everyone is with work and life, and that you may not have the time to pray. So I am doing it for you." My grandmother passed away in 1993, and those words still resonate with me today. To me, it's the perfect example of selflessness. That she would spend her entire day praying for the benefit of others and not herself amazed me.

Fast forward to 2004. I had been at my company for eight years. While we had always been a giving organization, our philanthropy was focused mainly on making charitable donations to a number of local nonprofits. Most of our donations were made out of our corporate headquarters. The leadership in our other locations oversaw charity donations to their local nonprofits, but no one owned the overall effort, and there wasn't a strategy or plan around it.

In the midst of this donation program, a small group of employees at our headquarters was taking it upon themselves to coordinate events aimed at boosting employee morale. One day, the Senior VP of Human Resources, who was my manager at the time, asked us in a staff meeting if anyone would be interested in representing HR on this volunteer team. I raised my hand and with that became the HR representative. When I joined the team, I learned that in addition to employee-morale events, the group also coordinated employee participation in a few charity walks from time to time. I went to one and observed that the employees who showed up really seemed to enjoy participating. There was a sense of teamwork and pride in representing the company at this event, however small the group was. So it got me thinking about all the great things we could be doing if we had a plan, a strategy, a full-blown program, and most important—a dedicated staff and budget for workplace giving.

I started to think about not just giving to but *partnering* with nonprofits to make an impact and help solve social issues. This, in turn, would create opportunities for skill development for our employees via volunteerism, raise the visibility of our brand, build our teams, increase engagement, and attract the talent we wanted. The best part, and what excited me most the more I thought about it, was that we'd be helping many other people in the process. I was all for that.

I knew I needed to develop a plan and that I would need the support of senior leadership. As a first step, I'd need to present my idea to my manager to get her support. But before I could do any of that, I had to prepare a compelling argument that the program I envisioned was a win-win for our company. To do that, I had to get a stronger sense of the company landscape: What did I already have going for me, and what potential challenges could I anticipate?

THE SCOUT MOTTO: WHY, WHY, WHY

Now you might be thinking, "I know my company inside and out. I work there, don't I?" How well do you know your company's purpose, its reason for existing? Knowing your company is more than just knowing what types of products you manufacture or sell, what kind of services you offer, or the benefit plan your employees receive. What you need to know are your organization's goals and objectives. You must understand your corporate culture, and why your company does what it does. In his book *Start with Why*, Simon Sinek talks about how leaders should look at their "why" first when developing their corporate strategy. The same holds true for your corporate giving or CSR strategy. Start with your company's "why" and build from there.

The reason it's so important to begin with understanding your company's purpose is because your program's goals and objectives will need to be aligned with your company's goals in order for you to create measurable and sustainable impact in your community and in order to successfully gain your leadership's buy-in for your plan. Leadership's support is critical. No matter how perfect your plan, it will never get off the ground without the backing of your executives. You'll also want them to be actively involved in supporting company-sponsored events, volunteer efforts, and fundraisers. Executive support and participation is critical in motivating your employees to get involved. It also shows the community that your company walks the walk. The best way to get your senior leadership's support is to tie your workplace giving or CSR program to your company's strategy.

Speaking of leadership, you should take the time to get to know the decision makers at your company if you don't know them already. What is their leadership style? Are they receptive to new ideas? What do they think about charitable causes and community service? It's time to start these conversations and ask questions. Think of it as a fact-finding mission to gather intel you'll use to create and deliver a watertight proposal to your leaders.

In *A Curious Mind* by Brian Grazer, he talks about informal interviews he's done with people throughout his career. He calls them "curiosity conversations." He credits these conversations with inspiring some great ideas for movies and TV shows, as well as with helping him make some important personal decisions. Schedule some "curiosity conversations" with your key leaders. These are the influencers in your organization—those who make the decisions on strategy and funding. Get to know what their priorities are. It will help you gauge how receptive they'll be to your plan, then adjust accordingly. You'll approach these conversations in different ways, depending on your role and position within your company.

ASK AND YE SHALL RECEIVE, THEN ASK SOME MORE

When I went on my fact-finding mission, I was working in human resources in the learning and development department. As such, I had access to leaders across the organization who were able to provide me with a lot of the information I needed. If you're in an HR leadership role, you'll be able to tap your senior leaders for their input and for the data you need. If you're not in human resources, a good place to start having a conversation about starting a charitable giving program would be with your **HR leaders**. First find out what, if anything, your company is currently doing on the philanthropy front.

Some questions you might ask your HR executive are:

- Do we currently support any charitable causes?
- Do we have a matching-gifts program?
- Are employees able to volunteer on company time?

If the answers to any of these questions are yes, then probe some more and get details. The more details you have, the better. This information will help you determine where your focus should be as you develop your strategy. If an HR executive answers no to some or all of your questions, ask the following:

- Has the company considered having a formal charitable giving program?
- Are there plans to develop a volunteer program in the future?
- May employees suggest charities for the company to donate to?

The answers to these questions will help you gauge receptiveness to the idea of a workplace charitable giving program. If nothing else, it will let you know how much convincing you'll need to do.

Your colleagues are another excellent resource, and knowing what they think will help you build your case. As we mentioned in the previous chapter, the feeling of being a part of something bigger and doing meaningful work is a key driver of engagement. Charitable giving and CSR help strengthen the connection between employees and their company. So you'll definitely want to include employee feedback as part of your argument for a charitable giving program. It will also help you determine the type of program that would be best received by employees. Once your program launches, you'll need supporters, and showing your peers that you value their thoughts and opinions early on will help create that support team. Those supporters will play a key role throughout your process, from program launch to embedding giving into your company culture. Tell a group of your peers about your idea and ask them if you can pick their brains a bit. If your company is already doing some charitable giving, ask:

- What do you think about our charitable giving program?
- If we had the opportunity to volunteer, would you be interested?
- Is there a cause you are especially passionate about?
- What problem in our community today do you feel needs the most attention?
- In what ways do you think our company can help solve this problem?

If your company isn't doing much on the philanthropy front, or if you don't have any giving program at all, then ask:

- How important is it to you that a company gives back to the community?
- Have you worked at other companies with charitable giving or CSR programs? What did you like or dislike about them?

Through conversations and asking questions I learned my company was already making donations to charities, but that we had an opportunity to make a greater impact simply by aligning our efforts across our locations. I also learned more about the history of the small team of employee volunteers I had joined. The concept of this team was great, but without a clearly defined mission, plan, and purpose—not to mention a budget—they were very limited in what they could do. I made a note to build the team into my plan, with the intention of expanding it and its role within the organization.

About budgets: If you're not in a management or HR position that will give you access to budget information, then simply asking if there *is* a budget dedicated to charitable donations in your company is a good start. A finance leader may not be able to share actual dollar figures with you, but they can confirm whether or not your company has a charitable giving budget set aside.

Begin at the beginning: If you're starting your program from scratch (which is where I was starting from), you'll probably want to hold off on going the full CSR route, as that would be like going from a bicycle to a Ferrari, and it's likely to get nixed by your leaders. Instead, start small. Identify the resources you already have at your disposal, and build from there. The big splashes will come later. Remember that this is a marathon, not a sprint. If you want leadership to buy into your idea, you have to show that it's doable, and more important, that it's doable without breaking the bank. Remember, we're going for a million dollars' worth of positive, impactful change without having to actually spend a million dollars to achieve it!

At my company, I wanted to build on our existing foundation of involvement by introducing a volunteer program, cause work via partnerships with nonprofit organizations, a formal grant-writing process, and a dedicated staff and department to oversee it all. Of all the things on my list, I knew the hardest sell would be the last one—creating a department with a dedicated, full-time staff to oversee our activities. It would probably mean adding to our head count, and that would cost money. Or would it? I started thinking about which internal resources we could tap in the event that we didn't get approval to hire staff, and I built that into my plan. (I'll focus more on resources in chapter 5, "Go Fund Me!")

By asking questions and having conversations, I was able to gather a lot of information on my company's position when it came to charitable giving. I learned that supporting our community was one of our core values. I learned that this dated back to our founder and his desire to do great things for the world by giving back to the communities where we live and work. I learned that our founder was very philanthropic in his personal life, which supported my argument for creating a formal giving program at the company. As it turned out, my "curiosity conversations" proved essential in helping me discover what I had going for me, and what I was going to need to work hard to overcome to earn buy-in from leadership. Working in my favor: our legacy of giving back, and the fact that we were already giving to some charities. And then the hurdles: we had no dedicated budget for charitable giving, formal program, or process, and the perception was that we would need to invest a lot of money to do it the "right way." Those were a lot of hurdles, for sure, but knowing this helped me to really focus on which areas I'd need to back up with data to make a compelling argument.

If you discover your company isn't doing anything on the charitable front, or that the extent of their giving program is limited, you're going to have a little more to do in the way of convincing your leadership to buy into your idea. You'll need to rely heavily on research, case studies, and best practices companies with established programs follow.

CASING CASE STUDIES

Part of my fact-finding mission involved interviewing companies with established charitable giving or CSR programs, specifically those I'd describe as best in class. Even though I had the advantage of working for a company that was already at its core a supporter of "giving back," I was proposing something much more complex that would require an investment of time, resources, and, yes, money to establish. Whether you have the advantage of working for a caring company or not, you need to include data as part of your proposal. Don't just quote statistics from articles and reports. Actual case studies must be a part of your presentation.

Talk to companies that have programs in place and find out what makes their program work, the impact they've had on their culture and their people, the benefits they've seen from having a charitable giving or a CSR program, and what you need to look out for. In the next chapter, we'll go through some sample questions. You should include a variety of companies on your list of interview candidates. I interviewed companies both in my industry and outside my industry, smaller and larger. You should aim to have at least five companies on your interview list.

Key takeaways from this chapter:

- Learn your company's "why"
- Get to know influencers and talk to peers
- Interview companies with "best in class" giving programs
- It's a marathon, not a sprint

CASE STUDY

Turning Business into a Force for Good: Causely's Mission

Causely is a Kentucky-based company that offers social-media marketing for small businesses—with one major difference. Every social-media check-in to a client by one of their customers triggers a donation from Causely to a charity. The client promotes their favorite charity with tools that Causely provides, allowing a client to differentiate themselves from competitors with their concern for a social issue.

Each month, donations go out to different charities, and the results have been incredible. Causely's 2016 giving included funding for over 21,017 winter coats and 38,263 pairs of shoes through Soles4Souls, more than 282,000 minutes of autism therapy through The Autism Site, and 245 sight-restoring surgeries through Watsi. Causely's website lists each of the organizations benefiting from their giving by month on a "Wall of Giving."

Another way that Causely gives back is through their #OneMore Movement. Visitors are invited to sign up for their blog and to join a movement within seconds of landing on their page, and their invitations are very inviting indeed. For each person who joins, Causely donates a meal to a child through feedONE.

Causely's perspective on philanthropy goes beyond financial commitments but well into participation and volunteerism. Their take on volunteerism is to cast it in historic terms, to call it a *movement*.

I love what Causely does for two reasons: One, I admire their innovative use of social media to make a difference. They've tapped into social platforms' potential for uniting people behind a cause. Two, they engage their clients in giving back while at the same time raising awareness about the untapped potential of the business community to change the world.

CHAPTER 3

GATHER INTEL

When I decided that I was definitely going to go forward with developing a plan and presenting it to my company's leaders, I was both excited and terrified. I was excited because I knew it had the potential to be really impactful, to engage our employees and energize our corporate culture like never before. At the same time, I was petrified that I'd be rejected or, worse, laughed out of the boardroom. I was determined not to let the second scenario happen, and I knew that in order to avoid becoming a laughingstock, I had to make sure I had a strong argument with solid data to back it up.

The good news for you is that there's a lot more information out there now than there was back in 2004 when I was conducting my research. The last decade has seen more and more companies promoting their good works and including their philanthropy and CSR activities in their annual reports. The advent of social media has provided us with ways to share a tremendous amount of data in real time. Social media is filled with groups and group chats dedicated to corporate giving and CSR. People discuss best practices, brainstorm ideas, and share experiences. Consumers, employees, and shareholders are increasing pressure on businesses to adopt CSR programs, and so there is a wealth of information out there now on what companies are doing.

I spent hours and hours researching. I didn't do it on company time, though. At the time, I had a full-time job as an instructional designer and training facilitator. So I did my research during lunch and in the evenings, long after everyone had gone home. Some nights I'd go home and continue researching into the wee hours. I was determined to gather as much information as possible so that I could make a bulletproof presentation.

As I thought about what I wanted to accomplish, I determined that what I wanted most of all was to make this program hands-on. I didn't want it to be just about sending out donation checks (what's known as "checkbook philanthropy"). I spent months gathering information on what successful and impactful corporate giving programs looked like. Boston College's Center for Corporate Citizenship was and is a great resource. There are endless research papers, articles, blogs, and reports filled with valuable data supporting the case for philanthropy and CSR in business. Search for CSR blogs and join social-media groups on the topic to learn about what other companies are doing. LinkedIn has many groups you can join, and other platforms like Facebook and Twitter often host chats that you can participate in. These groups allow you to tap into the most current trends and information, and connect you to experts in the field of corporate philanthropy and CSR. It's also a great way to learn best practices from those who have been managing these programs successfully. Keywords like "charitable giving," "corporate philanthropy," "CSR," or "corporate social investing" will bring up a slew of groups you can join or pages you can "like" to get regular updates on trends and the latest information.

These groups provide an excellent forum for asking questions and bouncing ideas off people who have created or now lead their companies' philanthropic activities. In participating in social media, you'll gain valuable insight into what works, what doesn't, and what to watch out for. Cone Communications is another great resource. They've done extensive research on CSR and cause marketing, and have many reports that you can easily find online. Take the time to do your research up front. Gather as much information as you can, and then choose the data that best supports your argument.

Most important, make sure that your vision for the program aligns with the vision, goals, and strategy of your company. If you think I've repeated that many times, you're right, and it's by design. I can't say it enough. Your ability to gain leadership buy-in for your program depends on it. It's *that* important. That's why those conversations with your leaders and influencers are key. Those meetings will help you extract the most relevant information from the piles of data that you will accumulate in your research. Homing in on what is important to your leadership team will resonate with them later when you make your case.

As for case studies, it's important to be prepared on that front as well. When I was researching companies to interview, I searched online for companies that had been recognized for their philanthropy or their CSR programs. People are very busy, and time is a precious commodity these days. If they feel like you are wasting their time, they will not want to speak with you. So have an agenda and go in with a plan. Create a list of questions before you call. You might want to send an email beforehand, introducing yourself and telling the person you wish to interview about your project, your goals, and what you want from them. Let them know what your purpose for reaching out is. Tell them that you will follow up the email with a call in the next few days. This way they will know who you are and why you are calling before you call, and there's less chance you'll be "screened" through an assistant or other department. Make a list of everything you want to learn more about, then go back and review your list of questions and narrow it down to a reasonable number. No more than eight questions. If you are able to secure an in-person meeting (which I highly recommend if the organization you are interviewing is local), it should be no longer than an hour. You might consider inviting the person to lunch.

> Tip: A simple Google search on "best corporate citizens" will get you a bunch of interview candidates. I looked at companies across industries and of various sizes. I selected local organizations and those outside of New York. There were ten on my list. I gathered information on all ten, and I interviewed three. Two were phone interviews, and one was an in-person interview.

RECOMMENDED INTERVIEW QUESTIONS:

- How long have you had a program?
- How did your program start?
- Who oversees the program?
- What guidelines did you use in determining your approach to grant giving?
- What other resources did you utilize in creating your program?
- Did you ask your leaders for input?
- Did you use employee volunteers to help plan some of your early events?

- What internal and external benefits have you realized as a result of this program?
- What are some of the challenges you've encountered in developing and/or implementing your program?
- What advice would you give to someone who is thinking of starting a philanthropy or CSR program at his or her company?

If you already have a program in place and are looking to make it more robust, then you would ask slightly different questions focused on how you can expand your program to include some of the facets of theirs.

Tip: Be aware that if you are calling a competitor, or if a company considers your company "the competition," they will likely not be as forthcoming with their advice, for obvious reasons. They may not even take your call. Do not rush this part of the process. Devote the time to gathering information on these companies, and especially to doing these interviews. Interviews are key because the data is "real time." White papers may be several years old by the time you find them online, but the intel you gather from these interviews is current, and that's compelling.

STEPPING UP TO THE MOUND

By the time I'd completed my interviews, I'd amassed quite a bit of information. Between the conversations with my peers and leadership, the research I'd done online, and the interviews with the companies I'd selected for case studies, I had literally piles of paper on my desk. Now came the fun part. I had to go through and determine what was key to my pitch and what wasn't really relevant. As I prepared my pitch, I considered my big advantage:

that there was some philanthropic activity taking place in some of our locations already, and that giving back was something that was important to our founder. So I used that as a starting point for my proposal. I drafted a white paper that covered the following:

Where We Are Today: Current State

This is where I laid out what our company was already doing on the philanthropy front. I listed the locations that were making donations, what types of charities we were donating to, and how often. I also listed the pros and cons of the structure.

The pros were:
- We were doing something
- What we were doing was aligned with our core values and culture

The cons were:
- There was no alignment across our locations
- No formal giving strategy
- No tie-in to company business strategy
- No dedicated resource or ownership for these activities

Observations: Information Gathered via Interviews with Leaders and Peers

Under "Observations," I listed what I'd witnessed as a participant in some of the events that our company's volunteer group had put together. In addition, I included the feedback from the leaders and peers I'd spoken with. Everyone agreed that to be really effective and make a positive impact in our community, we needed a formal giving strategy as well as a leader to oversee our philanthropic activities. All agreed that it required a full-time staff and/or a dedicated department to manage it.

Benefits: The Benefits of Adopting a Strategic Approach to Corporate Giving

In this section, I included the data I'd gathered from books, studies, white papers, articles, and other publications. Today there's even more information to be found via social media.

(This is also where you'd tie in your company's key business initiatives [e.g., employee engagement, recruiting, brand building] and present data on how a charitable giving program or CSR program benefits all three.)

What Other Companies Are Doing: Online Research and Case Study Interviews

This was a key part of my report and presentation, because I used it to benchmark our company against others. You can present this however you want—put it in a PowerPoint, a chart, whatever. I used a chart, laying out each company I interviewed side by side, including my company. Presented side by side in that fashion, this information made a pretty strong case for why we needed to adopt a more strategic approach to our giving. Most important was that the information in this chart was a real-time snapshot rather than a study published two or three years prior. I also included information on the other companies I researched that I had not done phone or in-person interviews with. The case-study benchmarking chart was the featured piece of my proposal and presentation to my manager, and later to executive leadership.

Next Steps: Short-term Goals and Long-term Goals

I broke this section out into short-term and long-term goals. I really wanted to put some points on the board early by including goals that were both achievable and wouldn't cost the company any money right out of the gate.

My short-term goals included:

- The creation of an interdepartmental group of employee volunteers—a community relations team. This team would build upon the concept of the existing small team of volunteers and would include representatives from all departments. This team would be key in helping to develop the program (and would provide me with resources in the absence of a full-time dedicated staff).
- The creation of an Executive Guidance Committee to review grant proposals and provide feedback on the program on an annual basis.
- The creation of a community relations charter with a mission statement, defined team roles and responsibilities, defined processes, and program details.
- The creation of a communication plan for sharing information on the company's philanthropy and other charitable activities both internally (email and company intranet) and externally (print media and Internet). This was in 2004. Today you'd obviously include social media, blogs, and other sites/apps like Twitter, Instagram, Facebook, YouTube, Facebook Live, and Periscope.

If you look closely at these goals, you'll see they have one thing in common: none of them cost any money to implement. Yet all of them would make a positive impact on the company's ability to extend its philanthropic reach further into the community and to build on a core value that had been part of our culture since our founding. The no-cost element here will be a big plus to your leaders.

Under long-term goals, I listed the items that would incur an expense:

- The creation of a formal program/department with full-time dedicated resources and a leader to oversee the program (expense=increased head count/salaries).
- Addition of volunteerism, a matching gifts program, and cause marketing.
- Corporate sponsorships and partnerships with nonprofits to create "signature" events for our company to increase brand awareness in the community.
- Evolution of the program to include our other locations globally.
- I had a timeline for each of these goals, spread out over a period of three to five years, with the less costly items taking place within the first and second year, and the larger items happening in years three through five.

Tip: Examples of things you would place in this category are specific sponsorships with nonprofits you identify as potentially being a part of your program, membership dues for community organizations that you might want your company to be a part of, salary for staff that you will want to hire to help support and run the program, and recognition items for volunteers (certificates or awards).

When I laid out my goals in this fashion, it became easier for leadership to embrace the plan because the expense was not being incurred all at once. Plus, the larger expenses were being deferred and stretched out over a few years, which gave us time to build them into our corporate budget.

Key takeaways from this chapter:

- There's no such thing as too much information—do your research
- Include case studies for benchmarking against your company
- Join social-media groups and participate in chats to gather information

CASE STUDY

Host(ess) with the Mostess: First United Methodist Church

When it comes to spreading cheer, First United Methodist Church of Shreveport, Louisiana, has found a way to make the holidays bright for those in need. For the last ten years, they've been hosting a holiday party for the residents of Greenwood Lodge, which offers apartments to Shreveporters with physical and developmental disabilities.

The church partners with Volunteers of America in northern Louisiana to sponsor and coordinate the party, which includes dinner and gifts for the residents of the facility. Volunteers of America reaches out to businesses annually to sponsor parties in homes for disabled veterans, people with developmental disabilities, and seniors. The church also serves their community by taking gift bags and companion animals to senior homes, reading to children in local schools, and knitting/crocheting "prayer shawls" for those in need of comfort.

Within the broader global community, the church makes an impact via mission trips. Church volunteers have worked with Costa Rica Mission Projects in San Isidro to construct new buildings and have supported clean water systems in Haiti through their partnership with Living Waters for the World.

Following First United's example of acting locally is easier than you might think. Contact your local chapter of Volunteers of America to partner for a community event, or plan your own event by partnering with a nonprofit or senior home in your area. Enlist your employees and coworkers to volunteer as hosts

and hostesses. It's a terrific way to give back and a real engagement booster!

CHAPTER 4

STRATEGY IS KING

However you decide to present your case for creating a workplace giving program to your manager and/or your executive leadership team (white paper, PowerPoint presentation, or both), one thing that must be part of it is a *strategy*. The proposal gets their attention, but it's the strategy that seals the deal. You can have the best pitch in the world, but you won't get very far without a vision statement, a strategy, and a solid plan to back it all up.

Before I go any further, I think it's important to spend some time discussing the difference between a strategy and a plan. Often the words "strategy" and "plan" are used interchangeably, but they are completely different things. Your strategy always comes before your plan, not the other way around. Here's why: Your strategy contains the steps you will take to achieve your vision for your program. Your plan is made up of the tactical actions that will support those steps. Think of strategy as the path that you will need to follow in order to reach your vision or your desired future state. So if, for example, your vision is to "Be the Customer's Number One Choice," the *strategy* encompasses the higher-level actions you would take to achieve that vision.

Examples of strategic actions:

- Capture Their Hearts
- Lead in Inventory
- Beat the Competition to the Customer's Doorstep

Your *plan* is made up of the specific tactical actions that will support the strategy. These tactical actions include the specific initiatives, teams, and plans to support each strategic goal. Here are some examples:

Capture Their Hearts (Strategic Action #1)

- Provide superior customer service (tactical action or plan)
  - Reduce wait time
  - Reduce number of dropped calls
  - Hire ten additional call center employees by third quarter to handle call volume
- Offer incentives (tactical action or plan)
  - Implement a "cash back bonus" program for loyal customers
  - Introduce free shipping on orders over $200

Lead in Inventory (Strategic Action #2)

- Expand product offering (tactical action or plan)
  - Identify top-selling lines
  - Add products not currently offered to complete the product line

Beat the Competition to the Customer's Doorstep (Strategic

Action #3)

- Invest in technology upgrades for faster delivery (tactical action plan)
  - Pilot drone delivery system in third quarter

Here are some questions you might consider when developing the strategy for your program:

- What is your vision for this program?
- Does your program's purpose reflect your company's purpose?
- What do you wish to accomplish?
- Where will you focus your giving? (Health and human services? Education? Environmental sustainability?)
- Will you brand your program with a special name or tagline?
- Is there a specific issue you want to solve in your community? (Hunger? Illiteracy? Homelessness? Education?)
- What do you need to do to achieve your desired outcome?

THE BEST-LAID PLANS

You've articulated your vision and mapped out a strategy that you're satisfied reflects your vision for your program. Now it's time to lay out the path that you will follow in order to achieve that vision. That path is your plan.

Ask yourself these questions when developing your plan:

- What specific actions do we need to take to support our strategy?
- Short-term goals?

- ▪ Long-term goals?
- ▪ What is the timeline for these actions to take place?
- ▪ What resources will I need to support these action plans? (People, money, inventory.)

FINDING YOUR FOCAL POINT

Part of your strategy will be determining the types of nonprofits that you'll be working with to support your vision and what you wish to accomplish with your program. Before you begin the process of looking into nonprofits to partner with, you'll need to determine what your program's focus will be. For example, will your program center around education? Or will it be environmental causes? Or maybe it's children's causes?

For branding purposes, you should look to align your program's focus with the type of business you run. For example, if you are a supermarket, restaurant, or in the food-service industry, you may want to partner with food shelters, homeless shelters, soup kitchens, or food rescue organizations. If you're a tech company, you might consider partnering with schools or nonprofit organizations in underserved communities to help create programs that provide students with the tools and technology they need to be successful. You may also consider donating your expertise and talent to help with skills training that is otherwise unavailable to this demographic of the population.

Choose one area of focus and brand your program around that. If you can't narrow it down to just one, then make it two, but ideally no more than three. This doesn't mean that you'll never consider partnering with other organizations outside of these guidelines, but those will be exceptions. Building your program around your area of focus will keep your program grounded, communicate a consistent and easy-to-remember message, and provide clear guidelines to help manage the expectations of the many organizations that are seeking funding.

After you lock in your areas of focus, you're ready to establish the criteria you'll use for vetting nonprofit organizations and to start looking into organizations that fit that criteria. You'll need to do your due diligence to ensure that the organizations you are partnering with do not have any questionable business practices, bad press, or, worse, issues with the law. Today there's plenty of information online, and sites like Charity Navigator and GuideStar even rate nonprofits. That being said, you should not rely solely on the information you find online. Plan to visit these organizations if they're local. If they're not, set up phone or Skype meetings with their CEOs. You should use the same process you used to gather the intel about your environment back in chapter 2. Conduct interviews with the leaders of these organizations and arrange to get a tour of their facilities if possible. Learn as much as you can about their operations: who they serve, their leadership, their track record for achieving their goals, their ability to be transparent, how your contribution will be applied toward their mission, etc.

More mythbusting: I'd like to address another myth here—that a nonprofit should not be spending money on staffing and salaries, and should instead put all of the money they raise into their programs. This view is not only unrealistic, it's unfair. In order to effectively run their programs, nonprofits need to hire skilled staff. They need to employ knowledgeable, professional, and talented individuals to help them drive their missions and obtain critical funding for research. Anyone who's ever recruited for a job knows that finding highly skilled talent is not easy, nor is it cheap. As with just about anything in life, you get what you pay for. Granted, you don't want to see an organization spending donation dollars on frivolous things or expenses that are not at all related to their mission; but when it comes to staffing, you don't want them to cut corners either. I'll elaborate more on this in chapter 10, "Seeing Double."

A nonprofit should be able to provide data and share examples of the specific populations they work with. Who benefits from their programs? Both they and you should know. "You are the company that you keep" holds true in business as well as in personal relationships, so you want to make sure that whomever you partner with has a great reputation, as it will ultimately reflect on your company. Review their financials. This information can be found online on their site, on charity rating sites like Charity Navigator and GuideStar, or provided by the charity itself via their annual report and IRS Form 990. An IRS Form 990 is filled out annually by most tax-exempt organizations. It gives the IRS an overview of an organization from an activities perspective and also very detailed information on finances and governance.

Be sure to perform the due diligence up front to ensure that there is nothing negative associated with the organization before. If everything checks out OK, the next step is an in-person meeting.

Many times, nonprofits will come in with beautiful marketing pieces containing glossy folders and colorful brochures, and they will immediately launch into the sponsorship opportunities and the levels of exposure you can get for your contribution. What you should ask for instead is examples of how they're helping people through the services and programs they provide. Ask them to share their success stories. Inquire about the challenges they face in trying to achieve their mission.

You should have a discussion about the specific role your company will play in helping them to overcome those challenges. Today's corporate funders want to have an active role in solving the economic, social, and environmental issues in the communities where we live and work. A nonprofit that is committed to a partnership with a corporation will be able to articulate exactly how your company would assist them in achieving their mission. If they can't, you should view that as a warning flag and pass on the partnership.

As you develop your own list of partner-organization criteria, you'll want to share this with your leadership team. They will want to know how you will determine which organizations make the cut for funding. Some of the criteria will be driven by your area(s) of focus, and some will be based on your company's mission, values, and culture. Be strategic in your selection. Look for opportunities where you can create signature programs or obtain exclusive sponsorship for a program. Enlist your volunteer planning team (more on them in the next chapter) to help you determine the criteria you'll establish for vetting organizations. We'll discuss exclusive sponsorships and signature programs in more detail in chapter 7, "Charter Your Course."

Key takeaways from this chapter:

- Your strategy always comes before your plan
- Align your program's focus with your business
- You are the company you keep—do your nonprofit due diligence

CASE STUDY

GROWing Better Communities: Advantis Credit Union

In 2015, Advantis Credit Union of Portland, Oregon, received *Portland Business Journal*'s Corporate Philanthropy Award in the Small Business Category—for the sixth consecutive year. Advantis has a remarkable eighty-five-year history of giving back to the community. Over the years, they have developed a variety of ways to assist nonprofits by donating their time, talent, and funds to making a difference in the community.

In 2011, Advantis launched the GROW Community Fund, which provides grants to nonprofits to help them better serve communities. In 2015, Advantis awarded $50,000 in grants to six nonprofits. In addition, the company donated over $113,000 to various charitable causes via corporate sponsorships and contributions.

The company also provides scholarships to local nonprofit organizations and schools through Advantis branch scholarships and awards scholarships to credit union members through the Advantis Scholarship Program. The company's philosophy when it comes to giving is to partner with their employees, nonprofits, and community groups to address needs within their local neighborhoods. This is evident not only in the grants and scholarships they give out, but also in the time and talent they donate via volunteerism and the free financial education workshops they provide to the community. Remarkably, in 2015, Advantis employees volunteered 710 hours, and the company provided thirty-four free financial workshops that same year.

CHAPTER 5

GO FUND ME!

Next is the toughest part of any presentation: the request for funding. People often ask me what the "right amount" is when developing a budget for their program. They'll say, "How much should I aim for?" or "How much is too much?" My answer is always the same: It's not the size of the budget or the number of resources that you allocate to your giving program that matters. It's all about how you leverage those resources and implement your program. No two companies are the same, and so it's a matter of taking inventory of your resources and determining what works for you.

Plenty of books will tell you that a corporation should invest a certain percentage of its budget toward their corporate giving or CSR program, or donate a specific amount of money a year to charity based on its size and revenues. If I had listened to those people, I would have immediately abandoned my idea. That's why I never give a number. Because the goal is to do something. Something beats nothing, every time. Start small, and build from there. But *start*.

The first year I was developing my program strategy, I had—literally—zero dollars to invest. Because I couldn't spend any money, I decided to dedicate year one to laying the foundation for the program I envisioned in my long-term strategy. I used my small volunteer team to review what we were already doing as a company. Next we established the criteria and processes that we would use to manage the new, more robust program once we received funding. We developed the metrics we would use to track participation and success, and we planned how we'd promote the program among our employees. We knew that even the best data can't hold a candle to real-life success stories and feedback. To get these stories, we held some events (what I called "test pilots") aimed at promoting charitable giving, fostering teamwork, driving engagement, and gauging employees' feelings about it all. We held a food drive, a clothing drive, a school supplies drive, and a fundraiser at different points during the year. We also registered for two charity walks as a company team. All of the events were very well received by our employees and extremely successful as far as participation. Employees loved being able to take part in the activities, and I received many emails requesting that we do more. Our people expressed pride in being part of a team and in the fact that the company was taking on a more active role in supporting our community. I saved every email and noted the results of each donation drive. I incorporated this data into my presentation to support the request for budget dollars to fund the program. It played a key role in securing approval and funding. (Hot tip: all of the examples of "quick wins" I just shared cost us virtually nothing.) The fundraising events and the walks garnered big returns from an engagement and morale standpoint—and with little to no expense to the company and minimal resources required to pull them off.

> Tip: If you don't have a charitable giving program of any kind, and are not able to pilot events like those I mentioned prior to doing a presentation for your leaders, then just use the data you gathered in your research to support your argument for funding in your presentation. Plan to hold events like those mentioned the first year, but do so after you receive approval and funding for your program. And remember to plan for events that will require an expense in the future as part of the funding request.

Starting from scratch was tough when it came to determining how much money I'd need for the future, so I made a list of things we'd need to budget for first. Then I went back and filled in the dollar figures for each. The charitable grants were fairly easy. I went online, looked at various nonprofits, and called or emailed them to ask for information on potential corporate sponsorship opportunities. Naturally, they were very happy to oblige. I noticed that the funding levels were pretty much within the same range, so I used that information as a placeholder in my proposed budget. Determine how many grants (charitable donations) you want to give in your second year (remember the first year is all about doing things with little or no expense to the company), and then slot in the dollar amounts needed for each. Remember that corporate giving and CSR help to build brand awareness. So you'll want to plan and budget for items that you will need in order to help promote your company's brand while you're out there doing great things like volunteering and running 5Ks for charity. This is where having a marketing representative on your volunteer planning team is key. Make a list of promotional items as part of your long-term goals for the program.

Examples include:

- Team shirts
- Branded giveaways for the public at events
- Media/press kits
- Product catalogs (if your company publishes them)
- Banners and tablecloths with your company's logo on them for events where you'll be in a booth or a tent
- Event-planning expenses (venue rentals, tent rentals, entertainment, food and beverage)
- Press and media outreach

During that first year, as we were piloting our prototype program and I was preparing to present my plan for a formal giving program with long-term funding, my volunteer team and I spent a good six months reviewing existing accounting processes to determine what revisions we'd need to make to support a formal charitable giving program. We needed to plan for the tracking, collection, and processing of requests for event sponsorships and grants, fundraising donations, and in-kind or product donations.

To our pleasant surprise, we found that very little revision would need to be made in order to support our plan from a finance perspective. Aside from the creation of some new budget codes to differentiate donations from other expenses, we had everything already in place to support our proposed program and department. I made sure to highlight that in my presentation to leadership.

Tip: The less reinventing of the proverbial wheel that you have to do, the better received your idea will be. Aim for minimal revision of current processes wherever possible, unless the revision is critical to the success of the plan or is required for compliance purposes. Then, without question, revise.

Having representatives from the finance and audit departments on my volunteer team made what might have been a nightmare exercise much easier. We repeated this exercise with other processes I knew we'd need to have in place to support my long-term plan, and where necessary, we slotted in the dollars needed to support these activities: a communication process (internal and external facing), marketing/advertising process (for the creation of sponsorship ads and promotional materials), and so on. I made a list of all the processes I'd need to have in place to support and track the actions I was proposing in my strategy. I tapped the experts on my team, and we went to work on a plan. Review, revise, and, when needed, create the processes you'll need to support your strategy and your plan.

A word about the planning team: Their input is extremely valuable in crafting a strategic plan that takes all areas of the business into consideration. The volunteer team doesn't need to include everyone whose shoulder you've tapped and brain you've picked. It should, however, include a representative from finance, marketing, human resources, and recruiting. It should also include an executive-level representative to help provide insight on what senior leadership will expect to see in your plan.

Finding the resources to get your program off the ground is probably the second biggest challenge you're going to have to face. The age of the job description is behind us, and we now wear many hats at work. If you want your program to get approval, you're going to have to show executive leadership that you can launch it without having to invest a ton of money in added head count. That means you need to get creative when it comes to people, and you will definitely need more people. This is not a one-man or one-woman show. Developing, launching, and sustaining your program requires a team effort throughout. As we've been discussing, the best way to accomplish your program's community goals while also engaging your employees is to establish a committee or dedicated team of volunteers for this purpose and assign each member a specific a role. Our group was made up of ten volunteers. Each person brought their expertise, business acumen, skillset, and unique perspective to the table. We'll discuss this team's role in more detail in chapter 6, "You've Got Funding! Now What?"

Key takeaways from this chapter:

- Start small—the big splashes will come later
- Review, revise, and when necessary, create the processes you'll need to support your program
- This is not a one-man or one-woman show

CASE STUDY

Serving Up the Goodness: Timberland

Since 1992, Timberland has offered employees paid time to serve in the community through the company's Path of Service™ program. Full-time employees currently receive up to forty paid hours each year to volunteer. To support employees in using their volunteer hours, the company holds two global days of service each year: Earth Day in the spring and Serv-a-palooza in the fall. Earth Day projects focus on protecting and restoring the outdoors, while Serv-a-palooza projects focus on revitalizing communities in need. In 2016, the company expected over fifteen hundred volunteers in fifteen countries to complete more than fifty service projects as part of Serv-a-palooza.

Serv-a-palooza projects include everything from planting trees in China, to renovating and repainting a local school in Vietnam. In France, Timberland employees have worked on greening projects with local youth to encourage engagement with the outdoors. In the United States, employee volunteers have delivered care packages to the Manchester VA Medical Center in Manchester, New Hampshire.

To support Serv-a-palooza, Timberland's global headquarters in Stratham, New Hampshire, closes for the day to allow employees, partners, and community members to serve at seven locations throughout New Hampshire and Maine. Jason Blades, the community service manager who leads planning for the headquarters' Serv-a-palooza, notes the lasting positive effect that volunteerism has on employee engagement: "The best thing is that the positive ripples from Serv-a-palooza continue long after the day is over. The organizations we serve are better equipped to fulfill their mission, and our employees are energized by the difference they made."

The best part about volunteering is that anyone can do it, and any size company can incorporate it into their program. Volunteering works for everyone because opportunities to do good exist in every community. Whether you have locations in multiple cities or multiple countries, you can find ways to get your employees involved in community service projects. You can do this throughout the year, or set aside one week or even a day for volunteerism.

CHAPTER 6

YOU'VE GOT YOUR FUNDING! NOW WHAT?
(OR, YOU DIDN'T GET FUNDING. NOW WHAT?)

So, you've received approval and funding for your program. Congratulations! Now what do you do? Three words: take it slow. Resist the temptation to rush into rolling the program out across your company. I know you're excited and happy and relieved to have your program approved. And I know you want to run out and start changing the world ASAP. I understand you are dying to get the program off the ground because it's a call to action for your employees and a major morale booster. I know all this because I've been in your shoes, and I wanted all those things, too. But I can't stress enough how important it is to not rush with the rollout. The long-term success and sustainability of your program depend on a well-thought-out, methodical approach with a solid plan and flawless execution.

One of the first things you need to understand is that your program will be something new for your employees. Many people are skeptical of change, and it's often met with resistance, even when the change is for the better. So the first thing you need to do is adopt a change management discipline that will help you roll out your program smoothly. If your company already follows one, great. If your company does not have a change management model in place, or if you have no idea what the heck change management is, you'll have to do some reading before you can move forward with rolling out your plan. There are a variety of change management disciplines out there to choose from. The ADKAR model is one example. The Kotter Model created by John Kotter is also popular. It's really a matter of which change model best aligns with your company and culture. This is why knowing your environment as we discussed in chapter 1 is so important. We'll discuss change management in more detail in chapter 9, "Making It Stick." For now, understanding the important role that change management plays in helping employees embrace change and knowing what you may come up against will be helpful to you in planning your communication strategy.

The first year that we piloted the program in my company we did it in our corporate headquarters. We chose the headquarters because it gave us an opportunity to try out ideas in a smaller environment, among five hundred employees versus several thousand across the company. We figured that doing this would give us a sense for what worked and didn't with our employee response, communicating and promoting the program, and the types of events we got involved in.

What we learned with the pilot program was:

Long-winded messages turn people off. Communications need to be short and to the point. Time is money, and free time is in short supply. The longer your message, the greater the chance it will be pushed aside or only partially read. Less is more.

Email as the sole means of communication is boring and inef-fective. Back in 2004, there was no Facebook or Twitter, no In-stagram or Snapchat, and no YouTube. It's hard to believe there was actually a time without social media and apps! Back in those days, most of our focus was on finding creative ways to promote our program internally with our employees and externally via our website and media outreach (newspapers, radio, and TV). Over the years, this evolved into using the company intranet, social media, videos, company/brand ambassadors, and volun-teers to promote our program both internally and externally, ex-tending our reach across our organization and with the public. Using various modes of communication is critical to employ-ees embracing your program and the changes that come with it. People respond differently to communications, so changing it up is important. Some prefer social media and some gravitate toward video. Others like blogs. Leverage all of these in your communication strategy so that your message is impactful and resonates with all your employee population.

People are very passionate about their causes. Everyone wants the company to consider their personal favorite charity for fund-ing. This is understandable, as is asking the company you work for to help, knowing how charitable they are. Having guidelines for sponsorship and a solid process for vetting requests in place prior to launch is important to managing these requests in a fair, objective, and balanced way. We'll discuss this in more detail in chapter 7, "Charter Your Course." Establishing an Executive Guidance Committee to review and approve donation requests will help you vet the many requests (and trust me, there will be many) and eliminate, or at least diminish, the personal requests for funding.

People have many suggestions for how to make your program better, and they expect to be heard. Plan to provide your employees with an opportunity to voice their opinions, suggestions, and concerns about your program. An annual or bi-annual survey is a great way to ensure that you are in sync with what's important to your employees while also engaging them in the process. Survey platforms like SurveyMonkey, Zoomerang, and Polldaddy make it easier than ever to quickly create and deploy surveys and get results. Remember that surveys don't need to be lengthy in order to read people's pulse. An employee should be able to take your survey in five to ten minutes, tops. Also be sure to include a section for comments so that your employees can provide freeform thoughts and feedback. You always want to include an area for freeform text because the comments add more substance to the survey results and provide deeper insight into the ratings.

Managing a program across different departments is like managing a program across different locations—with the benefit of everyone being under the same roof. Executing fundraisers and volunteer events within one facility helped us iron out wrinkles and resolve issues with processes in a way that was manageable. It also provided us with experience that enabled us to help our other locations work through similar scenarios when we rolled out the program across the enterprise.

A word about rolling out the program enterprise-wide: One of the biggest lessons I learned in rolling out the program across the company a few years after the initial launch in our headquarters is that you can't have a different version of the program running in different places. A mistake we made early on when we rolled out our program was adopting a scaled-back version in our distribution centers. The reasons for doing so were valid, in that logistically we thought it might be hard to execute some of the events, like the volunteer opportunities. We thought these would be difficult to manage in our distribution centers given that the hours of operation were different than in our corporate offices (i.e., some employees worked shifts due to the nature of their roles). Boy, were we ever wrong about this, and our employees didn't hold back in telling us so. I welcomed the feedback and was thankful for it because it made us revisit our initial position; in doing so, we took a closer look at the logistics and the program in general and realized that with a few slight tweaks we could accommodate these differences. It made a big difference in the way our distribution center employees viewed the program, and participation has increased exponentially over the years since the change was implemented. So unless it is a matter of interfering with business operations, do not run different versions of your program in different locations. Your employees will feel like they are being shorted, and it doesn't bode well for engagement. If there's no way around it and your business requires you to have a different program for certain locations, then transparency is key. Let your employees in those locations know why the program is different. Communicating openly and honestly about the differences is key to maintaining trust and keeping employees engaged.

THE IMPORTANCE OF A CHARTER

Before you can go live, even with a pilot in a smaller environment, you need to have your charter in place. The charter (bylaws, playbook, process document, whatever you want to call it) is what your regional teams and any employee who has a question about your program will refer to. It will contain information on your program's structure, processes related to the program, criteria for vetting nonprofits and awarding grants, and a whole bunch of other information that we'll dive into in the next chapter. For now, just know that you need to have this document in place before you go live—even with the pilot—so that you can establish a solid foundation for your program and provide clear guidance for your fledgling volunteer team as they begin planning and executing your first events.

Having regional cross-functional (interdepartmental) teams of employee volunteers in your other locations will help you when it comes to rolling out the program companywide and ensuring that everyone is following the charter. What you call the teams is completely up to you. I've seen them called many different names. Some companies call them community involvement teams, others community relations teams, and others CSR teams. The name you give these teams is not as important as their function. These groups will be instrumental in executing your program consistently and engaging employees across your organization at every level. The teams also function as your program ambassadors. More importantly, they are your culture ambassadors and advocates of your brand both internally and externally. These are the people who will help your employees embrace the program and, more importantly, make it stick. In this respect, they are also advocates for and ambassadors of change.

Group membership should be open to all levels. We've had individual contributors serving on the same team with directors and vice presidents. Talk about engagement! It's not very often that this happens in day-to-day business, and it's a huge morale booster for employees. The team rotates out every two years, giving other employees a chance to participate. This also ensures that ideas stay fresh. It's a great short-term solution to staffing if you don't have approval for a dedicated staff. In fact, you should describe it in your plan as a short-term solution and include budget dollars for staff in your long-term goals. That being said, our team did so well that we kept it in place even after I had a dedicated staff. The engagement they generated and the assistance they were able to provide to me when rolling out the programs were invaluable.

Based on the success of the team, we decided to expand the model to our other locations. Eventually we grew to have regional community relations teams in our other locations, totaling eight teams and comprising close to a hundred members across the country. We'll talk more about these teams and the key role they can play in your program, as well as the criteria you should look for when considering members, in chapter 8, "Getting Engaged," and chapter 9, "Making It Stick."

MAKING THE MISSION STATEMENT

Now that you've defined the purpose for your program and successfully articulated the vision, you'll need to create a mission statement. Mission statements are very important because they help communicate said purpose and vision. Mission statements also ensure that we stay true to our purpose, and like a North Star, they help us navigate the ever-changing landscape of the world around us. The most important thing to remember about your program's mission statement, aside from the fact that it should reflect your vision and purpose, is that it should complement your company's mission statement. It should be clear, easy to understand, and easy to remember. It should be easy for anyone in your organization to articulate. It should not be so lofty that it seems unattainable. It should reflect your program's values, goals, and ethics (which are also your company's). And, of course, it should reflect your company's culture.

Jack Welch, the former CEO of GE, states in his bestselling book *Winning*, "the mission announces exactly where you are going, and the values describe the behaviors that will get you there." This part of the process requires a lot of reflection and cannot be rushed.

It's worth mentioning that no matter how gung-ho you feel, don't go it alone. In fact, this entire process of building a strategy should be done in a group. When I was developing the strategy for my program, I enlisted a group of people at different levels in my company to help craft our community relations mission statement, including our CEO, CFO, various VPs, directors, managers, and individual contributors. This cross-section of our employee population allowed for different perspectives, and each person brought a unique viewpoint to the table based on his or her experiences and position in the company. It took us months to reach a consensus, but when we did, we were sure that we'd created a mission statement that articulated our purpose in creating this program and function in the company while staying true to our corporate mission.

NO DOESN'T MEAN NEVER

So far, we've talked about what to do once you get your funding. Now what do you do in the event that you don't get your funding? It's a scenario no one wants to consider, but it is a very real possibility. Know that I'm sending positive vibes in the hopes you'll get approved and receive your seed money to start your program right off the bat. If only that was all it took! Unfortunately, sometimes all the positive vibes in the world can't make up for a bad economy or a downturn in sales. So what to do if your plan is turned down? Two words: don't despair.

There are still things you can do to get your employees involved without spending money. If your request for funds for grants and sponsorships or for things like T-shirts and event giveaways is turned down, go back and take those things out of the pilot plan. Talk with your leadership about the other things you want to do that don't require money. The volunteer opportunities, the fundraisers, the clothing and food drives. These are still great events that help make a difference and require little to no investment. Suggest doing these things as part of the initial pilot. Get a few of these events under your belt. Then survey your employees to get their input. Once you've gathered this data (after your first year), you can revisit your plan and update it with actual numbers and employee feedback. When you have an updated plan and a year's worth of data to back it up, you'll have a stronger case for leadership to give the funding a second look.

The important thing to remember is that no doesn't necessarily mean never. There were several things that I wanted to do right out of the gate that I couldn't. We just didn't have the budget for it, plus there were no data to justify the spending for things like a volunteer recognition program or cause-marketing initiatives. By deferring these bigger spend items a year (or several years, depending on how big the investment was) and focusing more on the short-term goal of launching the pilot program, I was able to get my program approved the first year and funded in the years following. Making the first year successful on a shoestring budget and, more importantly, generating enthusiasm among our employees at the headquarters location led to my being able to secure greater and greater funding each year.

Key takeaways from this chapter:

- Test in a smaller environment/location first
- Give your employees a voice
- Have your charter ready before you go live
- No doesn't mean never

CASE STUDY

Teaming Up and Making a Difference:
TIAA (Formerly TIAA CREF)

One of the best examples of giving employees a voice and an active role in shaping and sustaining a successful community involvement program is TIAA's Employee Resource Groups. TIAA is an unusual financial services company, because it is a nonprofit. It is a conglomerate of related entities created and designed to protect and extend financial resources for a particular clientele: educators. They are focused on diversity and inclusion, and their employees are charged with taking the lead in ensuring that these values endure in the company's culture. One of the ways TIAA maintains a sense of mission and unique identity for their workers, who could all seek higher compensation for the same work at traditional financial services firms, is through the use of the aforementioned Employee Resource Groups (ERGs).

The purpose of the Employee Resource Groups (ERGs) is to unite employees who share common interests, issues, and/or backgrounds. Each of the groups has a specific focus. For example, Young Professionals, LGBT, and Veterans and their Families are just a few. The groups are open to all employees, and employees are able to join any group(s) they wish.

In 2015, the company decided to refocus the groups and reached out to employees across their enterprise, asking them to weigh in about the ERGs. TIAA wanted to revitalize their existing seven groups and sought input from their employees in doing so. As a result, the seven existing groups were renamed and an eighth group was added. According to the company's website, the changes were designed to help the ERGs "represent themselves in the most engaging, consistent, and inclusive way." The result? The employee participation rate has more than doubled, with over thirty percent of employees now participating in one or more of the ERG groups.

TIAA considers ERGs to be a critical component of their diversity and inclusion strategy. The company believes that these groups help foster open communication and provide benefits to employees such as professional development, networking opportunities, and attracting and retaining top talent. The groups unite employees in helping to make the community a better place to live while also providing personal benefits to the participants. In turn, they make the company a better place to work, which drives engagement and contributes to its overall success.

CHAPTER 7

CHARTER YOUR COURSE

Assuming you've received the green light to move forward with your plans, and that you were also approved to receive some seed money to start your program, the next thing you need to do is develop your program's charter. This is a very important document because it basically serves as your playbook. Think of it as a document that anyone can go to for answers to questions about program structure, internal contacts, processes and procedures, grant submission and approval guidelines, and vetting criteria for nonprofits. Everything you ever wanted to know about your program is in this document.

If you're thinking, "Gee, this sounds an awful lot like the information I presented to leadership when I made my pitch," you're right. The difference is that your leadership presentation was high level, focusing on leadership's concerns (mainly staffing and budget concerns); this is for the broader employee audience, so it needs to include the actual nuts and bolts of your program. This is the document that your regional teams and basically any branch, facility, store, or office outside of your headquarters will use to run the program consistently and efficiently no matter where they are located. If you were to win the lottery and retire to your private island paradise tomorrow, your charter would enable anyone in your organization to take the proverbial baton and run with it.

Caution: Because the charter contains information related to your company's accounting, budget, and other internal processes, this isn't a document to be shared externally with the public. However, some parts of it can and should be shared—for example, the guidelines for grant giving and your grant application information. We share this information publicly in downloadable documents in addition to providing application forms on our website. We also provide it to our nonprofit partners. Doing this demonstrates transparency and helps nonprofits put together a compelling proposal. It also saves them a lot of wasted time and energy trying to guess what information is relevant and important to you as a funder.

Your program charter can be as simple or as complex as you want it to be. Ours included everything from our program's mission to its definition and structure. We even included the proper accounting codes to ensure that everyone was budgeting and tracking expenses consistently.

I can't stress enough the importance of this document. From an operational and audit standpoint, it ensures compliance and consistent administration of the program across your enterprise. Just as important, however, from an engagement standpoint is the way it empowers your regional teams to take ownership of the program in their locations. The program charter holds everyone accountable to the processes and procedures outlined in the document. It is an invaluable resource that will ensure ease of management and execution of key processes and procedures. This is critical from an audit standpoint.

Another key function is that the charter provides transparency to your employees, which builds trust in leadership. You can make it easy for employees to view the document by making it accessible via your company's intranet. Having this information out there for employees to access shows that decisions regarding grant funding are objective and weighed against specific criteria and guidelines established in the charter.

Keep in mind that the charter is also a living document. While the accounting and budgeting information will most likely remain consistent over time, other aspects of the document will evolve and change as your program evolves and changes through the years. The first iteration of the charter for the program I launched was written in 2004. It's been updated at least five times since then and will surely be modified again in the future as the program continues to evolve.

Our charter contained information on the following:

- Program mission
- Department and program structure
- Our teams (headquarters and regional teams)
- Program areas of focus (causes we support)
- Sponsorship criteria
- Grant submission, review, and approval process
- Budgeting process and related information
- Miscellaneous (internal points of contact, various policies and procedures related to tracking and reporting on funding requests received)

As I mentioned earlier, you can make your charter as simple or complex as you wish. Theoretically, these bullets can each be stand-alone documents, separate from your charter. We just found it easier to have everything in one document. We even made the budget codes and related information into a chart that people could print and put up on their wall for easy reference. Simple and easy to follow. That was the goal. No one has time to read through a doorstopper filled with complicated instructions and industry jargon. Short, simple, and to the point wins every time. Consider that you can also use visual components like an organizational chart to lay out the information.

Now let's take a look at each of the sections of the charter in more detail so you have a better understanding of the type of information that's included.

Program mission

Your mission statement. The vision, goal, and objective for the program. Remember that it should reflect and incorporate elements of your company's mission statement as well. The examples I've provided of successful programs from other companies at the end of the chapters also reflect this. Those that are most successful connect their business purpose with their giving.

Department and program structure

Describe the program—for example, who oversees it, who's responsible for administering it, other groups involved in the program, etc. Use titles, not actual names, as people may move on to other roles in the future or leave the company. This saves you from having to update the names and ensures that the structure always stays current.

Teams (headquarters and regional teams)

This section contains information on the interdepartmental teams (headquarters and regional teams) and their roles and responsibilities. This is also where you would include information about leadership of these teams. For example, who will be leading the regional teams? Will it be the facility manager in each location or a human resources manager?

You should also include information about membership such as the length of service that members on each team must perform. Will it be one year or two years? In addition, you want to include the criteria members must meet in order to be considered for the teams. First and foremost, you should look for individuals who embody the company culture and are passionate about community involvement, and you should state this as part of your criteria. Then include information about how much time they must allocate to member responsibilities. Do they need the approval of their managers in order to participate on the team? Must they be in good standing? And so forth. All of this should be spelled out in the charter.

You'll also want to list the specific roles and responsibilities each member will be accountable for. You may choose to assign specific roles (i.e., treasurer, social-media manager, logistics/event planning, volunteer coordinator) depending on how you would like to structure your team. However you decide to move forward, roles and responsibilities must be clearly defined.

Program areas of focus (causes you will fund/support)

You may decide that your charitable giving will focus solely on children's causes. Or maybe it's education. Or sustainability.

Whatever the cause, you'll want to state it here. This is also information you can share with the public, and you should. As I mentioned earlier, my company posted information about our areas of focus on our website for anyone to access. This information is important for nonprofits in determining whether there is an opportunity for partnership between your organizations. It's important when determining your areas of focus that you begin with your purpose.

I talked about the importance of knowing your company's "why" back in chapter 1. It's at the core of your success at every level, but especially here. How can your company's purpose help to make your community a better place to live? Do some research—a lot of it, actually—on your community. What are the biggest issues that your community is trying to overcome? Which areas of the population are most in need of assistance? Identify ways that your company's purpose can help fill the needs within the community. By linking your company's purpose to the need within the community, you ensure that you are able to affect the kind of change that is not only measurable, but sustainable over time.

This is also a good place to talk about volunteerism and what your process for that will be. For example, will you have a corporate volunteer program, or will volunteering be done strictly on your employees' personal time? You should clearly state whether your program will include volunteerism, and if so, include the process employees need to follow in order to volunteer. A good way to monitor volunteerism is to create a special code for volunteer hours that your payroll department can use to log the hours in your payroll system. This makes it easy for you to pull reports and track volunteerism year after year throughout your organization. Meet with your payroll department leader to discuss options and create a plan.

Sponsorship criteria

This is where you list the steps in the grant application process that nonprofits will follow when submitting a proposal to your company for funding. List specific documents that are required (i.e., formal written request, grant application, financial statements). You should also include the types of requests that your company has determined are not eligible for sponsorship. Be as specific and clear as possible. Transparency builds trust.

Like the areas of focus, you can post the criteria and the application process on your website as well, with the ability to download and print the information. Include the application for sponsorship that nonprofits can easily complete and email to you along with other required documentation. Include an e-signature option to make it easier to submit the documents.

You should set up a specific email box to manage proposals and other communications and messages related to your program.

Grant submission, review, and approval process

Detail the process for the review of grant requests. In other words, who reviews them and how often are they reviewed (monthly or quarterly)? Will there be a committee who approves the grant requests? If so, who will sit on the committee? Will it be a group of executives? Will it be a permanent committee, or will it rotate members? You'll want to include information on how the funds are disbursed. For example, will there be a deadline for proposals, or will you accept proposals on a rolling basis? You'll also want to clearly state this submission deadline on your website so that groups applying for funding are aware of it.

Budgeting process and related information

This is really the nuts and bolts of how the teams will budget for everything from grants to operating expenses, event planning, and supplies. Outline who specifically will oversee the budget for each of the teams in their locations. Work with your finance team to determine which processes are already in place that you will need to follow from a budget and audit standpoint, and which processes you may need to update or create in order to support your program. For example, are there specific groups you'll need to work with or reports you'll need to pull on a monthly or quarterly basis to track actual spend versus what you had forecasted in your budget? If so, include all that here. Obviously, this is internal information and would not be posted on your website or shared with anyone outside your company.

As I stated previously, we got really specific in this section and even included a chart with all of the different expenses related to our program and the specific budget codes for location and line items, and which group was responsible for each item. The chart was formatted so that it could be easily printed or pulled out of the charter for handy reference.

Communication strategy

How will you communicate all the great things your program is accomplishing to the masses, both internally and externally? This is where you describe what you'll communicate and how often. How does your company currently communicate information internally to your employees and externally to your other stakeholders? Be specific about the type of information that you will share internally and externally. You will work with your marketing and communications departments to develop this strategy. If your company is very small, and you don't have a formal marketing or communications department, then work with your HR department on developing the communication strategy for your program.

Communication is a key driver of engagement. Employees' ability to embrace your vision and your program's success overall is contingent upon a rock-solid communication plan. How you communicate your program's goals and objectives to your internal and external community will play a big role in your program's sustainability.

Directory

This section includes internal points of contact, phone numbers, and locations. It's important to make sure that this section is kept current. People move into different positions or sometimes leave your company. Make sure to update this section every six months to a year to ensure that the contacts are current. Nothing is more frustrating than calling a number and finding that it has been disconnected or reaching someone who says, "I don't do that anymore," and is not able to point you to the new contact. Providing good, accurate, and complete information builds trust in the process, the program, and the leadership.

Key takeaways from this chapter:

- The charter is your playbook. It allows your company to run your giving program with consistency across your locations.

- The charter is a living document that will grow and evolve with your program over the years.

- Transparency builds trust. Make your charter accessible to all your employees.

- With the exception of a few key pieces of information (the sponsorship criteria, applications for grants/funding, and the grant submission deadline), the charter is not public-facing as it relates mostly to internal company policies and procedures.

CASE STUDY

A Sweet Story of Social Entrepreneurship: Project 7

Project 7 is a specialty gum and mint brand. Founded in 2008 by Tyler Merrick, the company was recently listed by BuzzFeed as one of twenty-two charitable companies that give back to the community. Merrick is considered a leader among social entrepreneurs, and his company is finding a way to give back to diverse causes via their products. Project 7 partners with a variety of nonprofits both in the United States and globally to address seven areas of need:

1. Feed the Hungry: provides meals in US communities
2. Heal the Sick: delivers life-saving malaria treatments to those in need
3. Hope for Peace: promotes anti-bullying programs
4. House the Homeless: provides emergency assistance after a natural disaster
5. Quench the Thirsty: provides clean drinking water where needed
6. Teach Them Well: provides daily school education in developing nations
7. Save the Earth: plants trees for a healthy environment

Each product sold by Project 7 results in a donation to one of the seven areas of need, and every product package shows the specific area a customer's purchase will contribute to.

Do you have a product that could generate charitable contributions like Project 7 does? Think of how you can leverage your products or services to do good. You don't need to go as far as Tyler and choose seven areas. One area will do, particularly if you're just starting out. You can designate a percentage of sales from the products or a specific dollar amount. For example, you can say $1 from the sale of a specific item will be donated to a nonprofit you designate. If you don't have a very big budget, you can set a cap or limit. This is what is known as cause marketing. Studies show that consumers are motivated to buy products when there is a connection to charity or doing good.

Be aware that these types of efforts require written contracts or agreements between a for-profit company and a nonprofit that outline the specifics of the charitable promotion. For example, how long the promotion will run, how much of the sales will go to the nonprofit, etc. This type of promotion also requires legal filings or registrations in many states. If you are interested in pursuing cause marketing, talk with your company's legal team about what's involved. If your company is really small and you don't have an in-house attorney, then research the heck out of this topic online, talk with an attorney who works with nonprofits to get the details on what is required, and reach out to some companies that are running these types of programs for some insight.

CHAPTER 8

GETTING ENGAGED

One of the greatest benefits of a workplace giving or CSR program is that it allows you to engage your employees on a variety of different levels, which ultimately drives overall engagement in your company. This is really important because employee engagement is critical to the health and well-being of your company (read: *any* company). A highly engaged workforce is a CEO's dream. Why? Because engaged employees will go the extra mile to ensure that your company keeps winning. These folks want your company to do well because they understand that when the company wins, everyone wins. But unless your employees feel an emotional connection to your company, engagement won't happen.

Aon Hewitt, a pioneer in the field of employee engagement, measures engagement in companies using a model they call "Say, Stay, and Strive." According to Aon's model, "Say" measures how much your employees are willing to say positive things about your company. It tells you what your employees need in order for them to want to be advocates for your company. "Stay" measures exactly what you think it does, your employees' desire to stay with you. More importantly, it tells you what your people need in order to feel that they want to have a future in your organization. "Strive" measures employees' willingness to go above and beyond in their job functions and to perform at high levels of excellence.

A company that is socially responsible and a strong advocate of community involvement will have higher levels of engagement than companies that are not actively supporting the communities where they live and work. In fact, Aon Hewitt's June 2015 white paper, "Say, Stay, or Strive? Unleash the Engagement Outcome You Need," lists demonstrating social responsibility in the community as a key driver of engagement along with an Employee Value Proposition (EVP) and Work Fulfillment.

Now here's the kicker. A 2013 study conducted by Stanford Social Innovation Review surveyed over 170 executives from midsized companies (companies employing 100-5,000 people). The goal was to provide executives with action plans for integrating social good into the way they do business. What they found was that fewer than ten percent of companies in the midsized category used their community involvement programs as a way to drive employee engagement. Of the companies surveyed, forty percent said they measured their program's success by employee participation. But the most surprising statistic to me is that almost a third of the companies that were surveyed didn't measure their community involvement programs at all. The study also revealed that although the community involvement or CSR programs are championed by the C-suite or executive leadership, employee engagement in their CSR programs is typically weak. There are several reasons the study cites as possible explanations. First, many midsized companies do not have dedicated resources to manage CSR initiatives. Without dedicated resources and a strategy and plan, sustained engagement is pretty much impossible. Also, many companies in this group support their communities via donations. This "checkbook philanthropy" approach provides little to no opportunity for employees to be engaged in the program outside of making a donation. There is a lot of opportunity for engagement via activities like charity walks and 5Ks or volunteerism. Human resources and marketing departments can play a big role in helping promote the program and encouraging employee participation, sure. But having employee ambassadors throughout your company to help you promote the program really helps to drive engagement. It makes them feel as if they are taking a hands-on role in supporting the program and your company's good works, and that's very powerful.

As I mentioned in previous chapters, employees in general want to feel like they are a part of something bigger, and that they are contributing to more than just a company's bottom line. They want to feel that their work has a bigger purpose. Certainly Aon's research has proven that, and other studies support this as well. In her December 2015 article "The Power of Purpose: How Organizations Are Making Work More Meaningful," Alison Alexander wrote that "the lines between social issues and business are blurred. There is mounting pressure for companies to go beyond a basic standard of 'doing well by doing good' to operating with an explicit purpose: to make positive contributions to society." She goes on to say, "individuals are increasingly looking for meaning in their lives and, given the amount of time spent at work, it makes sense to look to the workplace as a source of meaning. Purpose in business is a growing trend that might actually shift our way of thinking about employee engagement." The article details a study that Alexander conducted on the definition of purpose in business using a sample of 233 corporate employees from 184 diverse companies of varying sizes and industries. The article discusses how CSR can influence employee behavior and that it is extremely important for organizations to understand how their employees feel about CSR and the amount of weight they place on their company being a good corporate citizen. This underscores the point I made in chapter 2 about the importance of gathering intel by talking to your employees. It is a practice that will serve you well as you prepare to launch your program and in the foreseeable future. Because your program will grow and evolve with your company, knowing what's important to your employees, and what makes them feel that they are doing meaningful work, will help you to develop a sustainable program that will resonate with employees and drive engagement for years to come. As Alexander further states in her study, "Corporate social responsibility can be a key driver of meaningful work and a defining factor of a purpose-driven organization."

Finding out what is important to your employees, whether through casual conversations or a more formal survey, is one way of engaging them in the process. Another way is to involve them in the actual execution of the program. The way we did this was via that interdepartmental group of volunteers I mentioned in the last chapter. This team began in concept with that small group of volunteers doing ad-hoc fundraising way back in chapter 2. I took the concept of that team and expanded its role and scope within the company. We formed an interdepartmental volunteer team of employees who:

- Served as ambassadors of our culture
- Developed community involvement programs that fostered engagement and promoted volunteerism

- Executed our CSR strategy
- Worked with similar regional employee volunteer teams to ensure alignment of purpose and practice across our locations
- Planned and coordinated community involvement activities

We piloted this team in our headquarters first, defining roles and responsibilities and promoting the team among employees to generate excitement. Based on the success and learnings we gained from this team at our headquarters, we went on to add teams at our regional locations in subsequent years.

There are many benefits to having teams like these in your company. First, it solves the resource issue. Having a team of volunteers ready and eager to assist you with these tasks is a godsend because, let's face it, resources are precious commodities in any organization. Most of us are doing more with less, so having a team like this makes it possible for you to accomplish a lot of good without adding to your operating expenses. Second, this is a fantastic way to empower your employees. Being a part of a team that is tasked with developing programs and activities focused on making the world a better place speaks to a purpose-driven culture. Providing your employees with opportunities that give them the sense that they are doing meaningful work is powerful. It is a key driver of engagement, as evidenced in the research and studies conducted by Aon Hewitt and Alison Alexander, among others.

If you decide to implement interdepartmental volunteer teams, it is important to remember that these individuals will be representing your company in the community. They are basically the faces of your company at community events. Therefore, great care should be taken in selecting members. You should make the team open to employees at all levels of the organization to join. You definitely don't want to exclude anyone. That said, you should have specific criteria that applicants for a position on the team must meet. These criteria should be shared with all your employees. This is important. As I've been saying throughout this book, transparency is key. You want all employees to know exactly what is expected of members of this team, and the process and criteria that are used to review candidates and select members. A good way to share this information with your employees is to create a community involvement space on your company's intranet and post all related information there, including the membership criteria for the volunteer teams. If you don't have an intranet, ask your HR leaders where you can post this information for your employees to access.

Be specific about your expectations for the members. You may want to note that applicants must:

- Have a firm belief in your company's purpose
- Embrace and demonstrate the company culture in their interactions with colleagues and external customers
- Commit to the team for a minimum of one year and no more than two years

Setting a timeframe avoids the scenario of people "dropping off" the team because they weren't really serious about it or because they were just trying it out to see if they were interested. It also prevents managers from pulling your resources because they are "too busy" with other projects. The key is to recruit members who are passionate, committed, and focused on the program and on making a difference. Setting term limits also keeps the team fresh and eliminates "lifetime" memberships, which give the impression of favoritism and diminished transparency.

You can set whatever timeframe for team rotation works best for you. By making the team open to employees at all levels, you provide individual contributors with the opportunity to serve on the same team with senior leaders. Being able to say that you've worked side by side with an executive on a project is a big morale boost for an employee. For senior leaders, it provides an opportunity to connect with employees that are not in their reporting line. In general, it provides all employees with the opportunity to engage with people they otherwise might not get a chance to speak with or work with during the course of their workday. Teams such as this create connections and forge relationships, which in turn foster teamwork and camaraderie. All of this leads to increased engagement and higher levels of retention.

The other great benefit of these cross-functional or interdepartmental teams is that they connect your employees across the enterprise. As any company with multiple locations knows, the further you move away from the headquarters, the more isolated and disconnected employees tend to feel. Having regional community involvement or community outreach teams helps rally employees around a cause and generates a sense of inclusiveness and shared purpose. This in turn lends itself to higher levels of engagement among your employees. Even if your company is smaller in size or only has one location, the team connects people around a common goal and cause—making the world a better place. Relationships are forged and strengthened, and camaraderie ensues, whether you have two thousand employees or two hundred. Everybody wins.

The other thing the teams come in handy for is implementing

the new policies and procedures you create and put in place to support your program. In this capacity, they are change agents, or, as change management guru John Kotter calls them, the "guiding coalition" that helps drive change in an organization and, more importantly, makes it sustainable. More on the role these teams play in change management in our next chapter, "Making It Stick."

Key takeaways from this chapter:

- CSR is a key driver of employee engagement
- Employees want to do meaningful work
- Interdepartmental teams provide resources with no additional OpEx

CASE STUDY

Leveraging the Great Outdoors for the Greater Good:
Patagonia, Inc.

A great example of a company that understands the positive impact community service has on employee engagement is California–based Patagonia, Inc. The clothing company, which is headquartered in Ventura, has found a variety of ways to embed corporate social responsibility into its company's culture.

Many people who work at Patagonia are passionate about spending time in the outdoors. They are equally passionate about protecting the environment. The company offers employees the ability to do both through their Environmental Internship Program. The program, which was established in 1993, allows employees to take up to two months away from their regular roles to work for the environmental group of their choice while continuing to earn their salary and benefits. In 2016, thirty-four individuals across twelve Patagonia stores took advantage of this program, clocking almost ten thousand volunteer hours for forty-three organizations.

Now, not all companies have the luxury to allow their staff several weeks off to volunteer. I get that, especially if you are just starting out on your mission to launch a community involvement program. Remember, it's a marathon, not a sprint. Start small. There will be plenty of opportunities and runway to grow the program. Of course, if you have the resources and ability to implement something like this right out of the gate, more power to you, and by all means go for it! For the rest of us just starting out, Patagonia has two other, logistically easier programs, Salmon Run and Bike-to-Work Week.

The Salmon Run started back in 1993 at the Patagonia head-quarters in Ventura and involves a 5K community run, with all the proceeds going to local environmental nonprofit groups. Fundraising walks and 5Ks are a great way to rally your employees around a cause. Whether your company hosts it or just participates in it, a walk event or a 5K is the perfect way to rally your employees together and do good at the same time. It's easy to coordinate, low on cost, and high on engagement. Everyone wins!

Bike-to-Work Week takes place every June. Patagonia employees ride their bikes to work as a way to raise awareness for the environment by encouraging sustainable commuting. This is increasingly popular among Patagonia employees, as evidenced by their participation numbers. In 2016, employees in Patagonia locations in Ventura, Reno, and throughout their retail stores rode their bikes 15,036 miles during the week. This number represents a twenty-five percent increase from the previous year. Talk about engagement! As an added incentive, each mile that employees rode during the week was matched with a $1 donation to a local bike advocacy group. An activity like this one is great on a number of levels. Not only does it raise awareness for environmental sustainability and generate money for a great cause, it encourages a healthy lifestyle. You can adapt this kind of activity to any cause or nonprofit. Biking to work can be used to highlight environmental sustainability around Earth Day, and you could follow Patagonia's example and donate money to an environmental group. Alternatively, you could use it to promote healthy living during National Heart Month in February and donate the proceeds to a health organization. There is no shortage of causes. The only limit is your imagination.

CHAPTER 9

MAKING IT STICK

Change. It's necessary in order for us to grow. It's necessary in order for us to evolve. But for all its importance, many of us are resistant to it. The very word tends to make people uncomfortable. Depending on the nature of the change, it can evoke feelings of stress and anxiety. Change represents the unknown, and to many, the unknown is scary.

You may be wondering why I'm devoting a chapter about change and how to manage change in this book. Quite simply, it's because you will be introducing something new to your organization with your program. New equals change, and all change requires a transition from what was to what will be. If you're thinking that you don't need to read this chapter because, well, this is a positive change as opposed to an organizational restructure or a change in benefits, think again. A change for the better is still change. Consider also that while the big-picture change you are introducing with your program is a positive one, the implementation of new processes or the creation of new guidelines and roles for people within your organization may come up against resistance. Hence the need for change management. Without it, you'll have a really hard time making your ideas stick and sustaining your program over time.

Transition, according to William Bridges, is the hardest part of the change process for most people. Bridges has spent the better part of the last three decades helping companies manage change. He's a consultant and internationally known speaker on the topic of change and has helped countless individuals and companies effectively guide their employees through the phases of transition that accompany changes in the workplace. In his book *Managing Transitions*, Bridges explains the difference between change and transition, focusing on the human side of change. He says that change is situational, citing examples such as a founder retiring or reorganizing a team and their roles within a company. Transition, on the other hand, is psychological according to Bridges. He explains that transition involves three phases people will go through at their own pace as they internalize the new situation created from the change. These are:

1. Ending, Losing, and Letting Go: letting go of the old way and people's identification with the old way

2. The Neutral Zone: the in-between time where you've let go of the old way, but the new way isn't yet up and running or operational

3. The New Beginning: when people become re-energized and committed to making the new change work

If you look at the three phases on the surface, you might think that the hardest part of the transition is Phase 1: Ending, Losing, and Letting Go. There is no doubt that Phase 1 is a difficult phase because old habits are hard to break, and loss of any kind is not easy. But it's actually Phase 2 that requires the most attention because this is a time of uncertainty. The old way is gone, but the new way has not yet begun. This is the time when people tend to jump to conclusions and make incorrect assumptions. The rumor mill goes into overdrive and stress levels rise. Sounds like a recipe for disaster, right? It could be if this part of the transition is not managed correctly, and yet this phase receives the least attention. It is most often overlooked or rushed through in order to implement the new process, new idea, or new beginning. And it's why so many changes fail to take root and so many promising ideas die on the vine. Don't gloss over the Neutral Zone.

Let's take Bridges's transition model and apply it to the task at hand, which is getting your employees to embrace this fabulous new program you wish to introduce to the company. The best way to approach it is to look at all the different groups that will be involved in helping you to launch the program:

- Executives/senior leadership
- Employee volunteers
- Communications and marketing
- Accounting/Finance
- HR
- General employee population

Each one of these groups will react to your proposal of a new program in a different way. Each will internalize what this change will mean to them in a way that relates specifically to their role within the organization. It is important that you are conscious of this and that you are prepared to help them manage through the transition from what was to what will be, paying particular attention to the "in-between," or Neutral Zone. Let's take a look at each group a bit more closely and go through a hypothetical scenario of what the challenges might be for each as you introduce your program to your company.

Executives/senior leadership: This group might be dealing with the uncertainty of whether the program will create extra operating expenses and, if so, how the company would manage that. Reinforcing how you will implement the program without a big expense to the company is key for this group. Involving them in the process is essential to alleviating their concerns. Having a committee of executives as your guidance team and sounding board is a great way to gain buy-in for your ideas and obtain support for your program. Your employees will embrace your program a lot faster and will be more inclined to participate in program events if your executives support it and play an active role in its implementation. Getting those early wins that we discussed in the previous chapters will also help alleviate concerns about budget and help your leaders embrace the changes that come with your program. Remember, too, that those early wins help you build a case for future funding.

Employee volunteers: This is the interdepartmental group that will help you manage your program. They will also work as change agents, helping the rest of your employee population "get with the program" (more on that later in this chapter). In order for them to be agents of change, however, they need to be on board themselves. This group will be wrestling with the uncertainty of their roles. After all, this is something new. There is nothing to compare it to, no previous team members that they can talk with about their experience. They are pioneers in a sense, and that can be scary. They may be wondering if this is going to mean extra work for them. They may be hesitant to volunteer if they think it will mean more on their plate or extra hours in overtime. Be transparent and clearly communicate your expectations for the group. Clearly defined roles and responsibilities are a must and will be key to helping these volunteers embrace their role with enthusiasm and commitment.

Communications and marketing: As we discussed in a previous chapter, a solid communication strategy is key to rallying the troops and building excitement around your program. Communication plays a key role in change management as well. Keep in mind that individuals in this department already have many processes to manage. Now you are coming along with your program, and the communication you will need to do around the launch and for the foreseeable future will involve members of this department . . . which means extra work for them. Having a clear vision for what and how you wish to communicate will provide your peers with a framework to build on. Think of ways that you can make the process easier for them. Ask them if there is anything that you can do up front when it comes to communications (perhaps drafting them and then having the team just review and send/post them to social media). Be open to their suggestions and be willing to compromise. Listen to their concerns. Be flexible, but make your intentions clear. Also remember to share your broad vision for the program with the team. Talk with them about the role you envision them playing in helping you to execute that vision, and how it connects back to your company's purpose. You should do this with every group that you will be working with.

Accounting/Finance: This group will be concerned with the possibility of adding more reporting or creating new processes and models to help track and measure the impact your program is making internally among your employees and externally in the community. In their defense, they probably will be the group impacted the most by the implementation of your new program, most likely because it will involve running new reports and creating new processes. Transparency is key. Never ever downplay the work that will be required in order to sell them on the project. Put it all out there. Be prepared for possible resistance. Understand this going in, and think of how you can help make the process easier. Work with the group to identify ways you can update current processes versus creating a new one. As with the other groups, communicate your vision for the program and connect the dots between your program, their role in it, and how it all ties back to your company's greater purpose.

HR: Human resources might be concerned with how the program will be administered. While you may have a volunteer team to help you with the task of planning and administering the program, your HR leaders, like your volunteer team members, will see this as new territory. They may worry that they will have to step in and help administer the program if something doesn't go according to your plan. Or, they may be concerned with the lack of historical data. The unknown regarding how the program will be received may cause them to be more involved than they normally would be (i.e., expect some micromanaging). It's important that you understand that this reaction is part of the transition phase and not a reflection of how they view you or your ability personally.

One way that you can help your HR leadership feel more comfortable with the unknown is to keep them apprised of your progress prelaunch and, more importantly, post launch. Consider setting up a regular meeting schedule with your HR leadership to update them on new developments and to share those early wins. As the program establishes itself and delivers more successes, their confidence in it will grow, and they will become comfortable enough to step back and provide more guidance and less oversight. Be patient and be open to their feedback.

If you decide to implement the Executive Committee, then your HR leadership will most likely have minimal concerns when it comes to program implementation, especially since an HR executive would most likely be a member of the committee. Nonetheless, having regular meetings with HR is still a good idea from a transparency standpoint.

General employee population: Your employees will have a lot of questions. Some of the questions I received before we even launched the program centered around the types of charities we'd support, if there would be opportunities to volunteer during work hours, and if we'd have a matching gifts program. It's important that you listen to your employees and be available to answer their questions. You may want to set up a special email for employees to submit questions and ideas. If your company has an intranet, set up a space where employees can sign in and see regular updates on program status and launch date. You could set up a countdown to launch with a countdown clock to build excitement. This shows transparency while also creating a positive buzz and engagement around the program. After your program launches, you can turn this space into an area where you post upcoming events on a calendar and share photos and highlights from different events, spotlight your nonprofit partners, and showcase employee volunteers. Create message boards and peer recognition areas to connect your employees to one another to celebrate their spirit of giving and foster engagement.

In all these examples, you might notice that the theme when managing the phase of uncertainty or the Neutral Zone is communication. Being as transparent as possible, being open to ideas and suggestions, listening to the concerns of all parties, and involving them where possible (and feasible) in the development of the program and related processes will go a long way. Be willing to roll up your sleeves and help wherever and whenever you can. This demonstrates an understanding of the challenges different parties may be facing and a willingness to alleviate their burden. When we were creating our program it was truly a team effort with all hands on deck.

Communicating your vision, expectations, and desired outcomes to everyone involved in the process builds trust and keeps rumors at bay, and this is key to employees embracing your program and the changes that come with it. It's also the key to making those changes stick. I mentioned the idea of a "guiding coalition" earlier in this chapter. John Kotter describes these individuals in his "8 Steps of Change" as "key change leaders." These are the people who will assist you in communicating your message and reinforce your program's mission across your company. It is a big responsibility, one that requires people who are strong believers of your mission and truly passionate about the cause. This is why it is important to choose people who are recognized as leaders by their peers.

My cross-functional volunteer team served as the guiding coalition when I launched my program over ten years ago, and this team continues to play this role today. They have been instrumental in driving employee participation in our program and in helping employees connect our company's purpose and strategy to our program. More important, they have helped our employees understand the role that each individual plays in helping our program support the communities where we live and work, along with our company's strategy. The group has also been great in providing us with real-time feedback from employees on events, fundraisers, and program implementation.

As Kotter states in his book *Leading Change*, buy-in comes in part by teaching new behaviors via the guiding coalition. Your employees will be watching this group and modeling their behavior. Ensure that the group is made up of positive, committed, and well-respected leaders who believe in your vision and what you are trying to achieve. Jack Welch also points out in *Winning* that great leaders possess what he calls the "4 E's and 1 P":

1. Positive *E*nergy
2. The Ability to *E*nergize Others
3. *E*dge—The Courage to Make Tough Decisions
4. *E*xecution—The Ability to Get the Job Done
5. *P*assion—Welch describes passion as "a heartfelt, deep, and authentic excitement about work." He says that "people with passion care—really care in their bones—about colleagues, employees, and friends winning."

Welch advises us to look for the "4 E's and 1 P of Leadership" when reviewing candidates at any level in an organization, because people who possess these traits build and are part of winning teams. If you find that a candidate has all 4 E's, he says to then look for the P. Why? Because as Welch stated in his 2013 LinkedIN article "How I Hire: The Must Haves, the Definitely-Should Haves and the Game-Changer," "The 4 E's are great individually, but they're even better when a candidate has them all wrapped up in a burning ball of passion—there's the P—for both work and life." The "P" is extremely important because, as Welch points out "passionate people sweat the details, they're curious, they care." Your volunteers do not have to have executive or management roles in the company, but they must be viewed as leaders by their peers. Rallying your employees around your program depends on it.

Key takeaways from this chapter:

- The transition is what gets people "fraidy-scared"
- Never underestimate the Neutral Zone
- Communicate, communicate, communicate
- Assemble a winning coalition of change agents

CASE STUDY

Leading the Way Through Partnerships: Levi Strauss & Co.

More than twenty-five years ago, Levi Strauss & Co. introduced a comprehensive code of conduct. Called the Levi Strauss & Co. Terms of Engagement, it set out to protect the basic needs and rights of workers as well as the environment. Since its implementation, similar codes have become the industry standard and are now employed by most apparel companies.

In 2011, LS&Co. began piloting the next phase of its commitment to creating a more sustainable supply chain called the Worker Well-being initiative. The company partners with its suppliers and local organizations to implement programs focused on financial empowerment, health and family well-being, and equality and acceptance. LS&Co. supports progressive leaders and organizations that take risks and innovate to address pressing social issues, from HIV/AIDS to human rights.

Worker Well-being takes a unique approach to addressing worker needs that starts with listening to workers. Before implementing any program or intervention, LS&Co.'s suppliers survey factory workers to get a firsthand account about what they need to be more engaged, healthy, and productive. LS&Co. and its suppliers then partner with local and national nonprofits and NGOs to implement programs to meet the needs of workers.

LS&Co.'s employees take a hands-on approach to supporting their communities as well. Employees across their locations globally have formed Community Involvement Teams (CITs), which bring the company's values to life in a variety of amazing ways. These company-sponsored groups partner with local charitable organizations to identify needs, plan activities, volunteer, and identify donation opportunities.

As an incentive for volunteerism, LS&Co. offers full-time employees up to five hours per month (sixty hours per year) paid time off to volunteer at a charitable organization of their choice. In the United States, the Levi Strauss Foundation matches employee and retiree contributions to qualifying organizations. In addition, the company provides grants to nonprofit organizations where employees volunteer on their own time. On a larger scale, Levi Strauss designates a Community Day each May. On this day, employees across the globe take the day off from work to volunteer with local nonprofit organizations.

Whatever the size of your company, there are plenty of great examples and ideas to draw from the Levi Strauss & Co. story.

CHAPTER 10

SEEING DOUBLE: NONPROFITS AND THE OL' DOUBLE STANDARD

If there's one thing that drives me absolutely crazy, it's the notion that nonprofits should not be spending any money on operating expenses. As a society, we expect these organizations to solve issues in our communities, find cures for diseases, and in essence change the world. We hold them accountable for achieving their noble missions and lofty goals, and yet we demand that they do this without spending a penny on the resources they need to make it happen. They are not allowed to invest in the staffing, training, marketing, or advertising required to attract donors or raise awareness—two actions that help raise funds to support community programs and create the change we're looking for. While it is understandable that we should want nonprofits to direct the funds they raise or the grants they are awarded to the programs and causes they advocate for, it is unrealistic to think that they can do this without spending money on overhead. The reality is that a nonprofit is like a business. It is in the business of supporting our communities. It is in the business of providing services and assistance to millions of people who are afflicted by disease, disability, homelessness, hunger, abuse, financial devastation—the list goes on. Yet we place so many restrictions on them that we make it virtually impossible for them to succeed.

We'd be considered certifiably nuts for even contemplating such a scenario in the for-profit world. Think about it. Imagine if a CEO was asked to fill executive-level positions in her company with volunteers? What if managers were asked to cut corners and settle for a candidate with little to no experience in the field versus hiring a seasoned high-performer? Or if the sales force was not permitted to spend any money on hiring extra reps or investing in marketing or advertising campaigns but was still expected to bring in new accounts and increase revenue. Yet this is exactly what we as a society force nonprofits to do. It's *Twilight Zone* bizarre when you really stop and reflect on it.

Dan Pallotta has been raising awareness about this double standard for years by helping us see the proverbial light when it comes to nonprofit operations. He's helping us rethink the way we view nonprofits and charity overall. Through his books *Uncharitable: How Restraints on Nonprofits Undermine Their Potential* and *Charity Case: How the Nonprofit Community Can Stand Up for Itself and Really Change the World*, he's brought this issue to the forefront of our consciousness. But what really captured the world's attention was his game-changing 2013 TED Talk, "The Way We Look at Charity is Dead Wrong." In it, he discussed the discrimination that nonprofits are subjected to and how this has prevented them from solving the most significant issues facing our communities. I highly recommend taking twenty minutes to watch it. It's a real eye-opener. In his talk, Dan poses a series of questions: Why have our breast cancer charities not come close to finding a cure for breast cancer? Why have our homeless charities not come close to ending homelessness in any major city? Why has poverty in the United States remained stuck at twelve percent for forty years? The answer, he says, is that there are different rule books, "one for the nonprofit sector and one for the rest of the economic world." He describes it as "an apartheid" that discriminates against the nonprofit sector in the following areas:

Compensation: For-profit companies are expected to pay their top producers in order to provide incentives for higher performance. Nonprofits, by comparison, produce what Pallotta calls a "visceral reaction" in society if they attempt to do the same by incentivizing people to do more in social service.

Advertising and marketing: While we understand that it is necessary for nonprofits to advertise in order to motivate donors to open their wallets, we expect that these services should be donated. We don't want to hear that our dollars went toward a marketing campaign, even if that marketing campaign could potentially attract a ton of new donors and raise a boatload of cash for the cause. We've been conditioned to believe that this is a bad thing and brainwashed to look unfavorably on nonprofits that invest in these types of expenses.

Taking risks in coming up with new ideas for generating revenue: According to Pallotta, nonprofits avoid daring fundraising ideas because of a fear of ruining their reputation if the idea bombs. So they are stuck in a rut of the same old outdated practices that yield mediocre results. Innovation is stifled and in most cases nonexistent because, unlike for-profit companies that are expected to learn from their failures, nonprofits are penalized when something goes wrong. As a result, nonprofits avoid taking risks and steer clear of attempting new fundraising endeavors because of the potential damage to their reputation.

Time: Nonprofits do not have the luxury of time that for-profit organizations have to strategize toward leadership. In his TED Talk, Pallotta uses the example of how Amazon went six years without returning any profit to investors, yet the public was patient with them because they knew that the long-term objective for Amazon was achieving market dominance. He points out that, by contrast, if a nonprofit had stated that all of their funding would be invested in building a strategy that would require six years to come to fruition, the public would, and I quote, "expect crucifixion."

Profit: Quite simply, the for-profit sector can pay people to attract their capital for new ideas, but the nonprofit sector is not able to do this. Hence, the nonprofit sector is at a huge disadvantage for growth, risk, and idea capital compared to for-profits.

As a nonprofit founder himself, Pallotta speaks from experience. He knows all too well that investing in marketing and trying new ideas in the hopes of generating revenue can draw the ire of sponsors, despite the genuine impact these investments have on fundraising.

Pallotta launched his AIDSRide with an initial investment of $50,000 in risk capital. Over nine years, this amount multiplied to $108 million after all expenses were paid. Likewise, he founded a three-day breast cancer event with an initial investment of $350,000 in risk capital. Within five years, this had grown to $194 million after all expenses were paid. In 2002, which Pallotta considers his nonprofit's most successful year, they raised $71 million for breast cancer. Now you're probably reading this and thinking, "That's amazing! What a great success story!" And it is. The trouble is that instead of being praised for their innovative strategy and smart investing, his nonprofits were penalized. In fact, their sponsors all jumped ship. As Pallotta said, "The sponsors wanted to distance themselves from us because we were being crucified in the media for investing forty percent of the gross in recruitment and customer service and the magic of the experience, and there is no accounting terminology to describe that kind of investment in growth and in the future, other than this demonic label of 'overhead.'"

Dan Pallotta's groundbreaking TED Talk started conversations both in and outside of the nonprofit sector. The buzz was big. Within three months of his talk going live, GuideStar, Charity Navigator, and the Better Business Bureau Wise Giving Alliance, three leading resources for nonprofit data in the United States, announced that they were "denouncing the 'overhead ratio' as a valid indicator of nonprofit performance." In fact, the CEOs of all three organizations wrote an open letter to donors stating the following: "We write to correct a misconception about what matters when deciding which charity to support. The percent of charity expenses that go to administrative and fundraising costs—commonly referred to as 'overhead'—is a poor measure of a charity's performance. We ask you to pay attention to other factors of nonprofit performance: transparency, governance, leadership, and results."

Great news indeed, but there is still much work to be done in changing the current mindset and creating one rule book for nonprofits and for-profits. Keeping the conversation going is critical.

As you begin your journey toward creating a charitable giving or CSR program in your company, it's important that you not fall into the trap of judging nonprofits by what Dan calls the dangerous question: "What percentage of my donation goes to the cause versus overhead?" I'll admit, when I first started out twelve years ago, I was asking that question a lot. But time, experience, and, most important, the cultivation of relationships with my nonprofits have helped me to understand the real struggles they face on a daily basis.

So raising awareness by keeping the conversation going is big. But taking action is also important. There are things we can do (and by "we," I mean corporate funders) right now to help our nonprofits while continuing to raise society's consciousness on this topic. Giving takes many forms. Volunteerism is a big way that you can lend a hand. Donate your time, expertise, and talent to help nonprofits accomplish what they aren't able to invest in because they fear the "demonic label" of overhead.

Remember Brian Grazer's "curiosity conversations" way back in chapter 2? Here's another chance to practice having them and to put them to good use. Have "curiosity conversations" with your nonprofits. Inquire about the challenges they are facing. What are their biggest operational pain points? What is the most significant obstacle standing in the way of their fundraising goals? Ask if there are tasks your employees can help with. Perhaps they need help building a website. Maybe they need someone to help them formulate a social media strategy. They may need help with bookkeeping or administrative tasks. Are there products or services you can donate? Most nonprofits are not able to invest in consulting services or training because these services are too expensive. Think about whether there are services such as these that your company can donate to a nonprofit. Many times nonprofits are hesitant to ask, or they might not know that they can even ask you for this type of help. Reach out. Inquire. You'll learn a lot, and your nonprofits will thank you for it. Solid relationships are founded on open and honest communication. What better way to start your relationship with a nonprofit than by having a candid dialogue and expressing genuine interest in not just funding their mission, but helping them to achieve it.

When the business community partners with the nonprofit community in this way, it's incredibly powerful and mutually beneficial. Businesses benefit from employee engagement and a positive reputation, which attracts favorable attention and top talent. Nonprofits benefit from support on a financial and operational level. But the biggest winner in all of this is the community, because in partnering, we are able to accomplish much more than we would individually. We are able to create sustainable change.

There are professional organizations that assist nonprofits via programs and workshops focused on creating strategies, building relationships with donors, engaging volunteers, and coaching and development for nonprofit leaders and their board members. These workshops and services help nonprofits build relationships with donors, which helps them achieve sustainable fundraising. Two such organizations that offer these resources are BoardSource and Benevon.

BoardSource is all about what they call "board advocacy and ambassadorship." They produce a biennial study, entitled "Leading with Intent: A National Index of Nonprofit Board Practices," which tracks trends in board leadership and governance. They've been collecting this data since 1994, and they work directly with nonprofit boards and executives. In 2014, BoardSource partnered with GuideStar to create a new portal on the GuideStar exchange that enables organizations to share best practices around board leadership, ethics, and transparency, among other things.

Benevon was founded in 1996 by Terry Axelrod, a professional fundraiser and social worker. Axelrod created a model for sustainable fundraising after having spent over thirty years working in the nonprofit sector. She served as Development Consultant to Zion Preparatory Academy in Seattle from 1992 to 1995. While there, she designed and implemented fundraising and marketing programs that yielded $7.2 million in two and a half years. This garnered national recognition for the program and for Axelrod, who was featured in a cover story in the *Chronicle of Philanthropy*.

Benevon conducts annual two-day workshops in various cities across the United States focused on teaching nonprofits how to achieve sustainable fundraising via a four-step process called the Benevon Model. Nonprofits bring a team of seven people to the workshops. These teams are made up of board members, staff, and volunteers. Coaches and instructors work with each organization over the two days to customize the model to meet their unique needs. As part of the workshop, each organization presents its model to the other attending groups who provide feedback and recommendations on the model. Since 1996, Benevon has trained over 4,500 nonprofit teams in the United States, Canada, the United Kingdom, and several European countries. All types of nonprofits have attended the sessions. If you're a nonprofit, check out their website at www.benevon.com for detailed information on their services and workshops. If you are not able to attend a workshop, take heart. Axelrod has written several books on this subject. Here are three you may want to read: *The Joy of Fundraising*, *The Benevon Model for Sustainable*

Funding: A Step-by-Step Guide to Getting It Right, and *Mission-izing Your Special Events*.

Key takeaways from this chapter:

- It's time to do away with the double standard
- Overhead is not a dirty word
- Giving comes in many forms
- Donating services and expertise goes a long way

CASE STUDY

Aligning Purpose with Partnerships: Jane Cosmetics

Jane Cosmetics is one of the best examples of the powerful impact that can be made when businesses align their purpose with the right nonprofit partner(s). Founded in 1994, the company makes beauty products sold at mass retailers and drugstores in the United States and Canada. The name "Jane" represents the girl next door and was meant to convey the idea that every woman can advocate for social change. In fact, Jane's philosophy is centered around enlightening and empowering girls and young women.

CEO Lynn Tilton acquired the company back in 2009 with the mission to empower women to be "confident, courageous, and socially conscious." Some examples of how this company is giving back include providing makeup services for underprivileged girls and partnering with organizations that hold special events for girls undergoing cancer treatment. Jane contributes time, services, and talent to the cause by deploying a team of makeup artists to the events to give girls makeovers. But make no mistake, this company is not about superficial beauty. On the contrary, it's all about promoting confidence and social good to cultivate inner beauty.

Another way Jane Cosmetics gives back to the community is through its "Friends of Jane" program. Jane partners with a variety of different nonprofits to promote a message of empowerment. In 2012, the company partnered with a fledgling nonprofit by the name of She's the First. The organization's mission is focused on educating girls in developing countries. This was a perfect fit with Jane's philosophy of empowerment. The company created a specially packaged lip gloss that mentioned the charity on the packaging. One hundred percent of the proceeds from the sale of this lip gloss were donated to She's the First. The company has also sponsored a fundraiser for She's the First, which consisted of engaging high school and college students from across the country in a bake-sale fundraiser to raise money for girls' educations sponsorships in eight developing countries.

The fundraisers took place over a one-week period in the month of November and were driven by social media. Students used the powerful platform, in addition to newspapers, to promote the fundraiser, which consisted of cupcake sales. Between 2012 and 2013, the fundraisers garnered $60,000 in donations. What's more, they engaged two hundred student teams via She's the First chapters in over forty high schools and colleges across the country.

I love this story because of all the wins and because of the different ways that Jane Cosmetics conducts community outreach and engages its employees in doing good, from donating time and talent to helping underprivileged girls and girls undergoing cancer treatment to feel confident and beautiful, to engaging students in an exercise that benefits the global community (and teaches them about entrepreneurship). Simple things, like makeovers and bake sales, make a big impact. As Lynn Tilton says, "Little things like that can go a long way." That's "Million Dollar" change!

AFTERWORD

My goal in writing this book was to inspire companies to action in supporting the communities where their employees live and work. There is a misconception out there that corporations provide the bulk of the donations that nonprofits receive. This is false. In fact, the majority of the donations made annually to nonprofits come from individuals. In 2015, a study by Charity Navigator revealed that seventy-one percent of all donations made to nonprofits come from individuals. If you add gifts and bequests from family foundations to the mix, which are essentially gifts from individuals, that number jumps up to eighty percent. What this says is that there is clearly a lot more that corporations can be doing to make our communities healthier, stronger, and more prosperous.

According to the Small Business Administration, there were 27.9 million small businesses and 18,500 firms with 500 employees or more in the United States in 2010. Imagine if each of these businesses had a charitable giving program. The impact corporations could make by working with nonprofits and community groups to solve social, environmental, and financial issues in our communities could be tremendous. Indeed, for decades, human resources professionals and business leaders have been alert to the importance and impact of corporate social responsibility. Numerous articles, white papers, and books discuss why it's in a company's best interest to adopt charitable giving as part of a business strategy. Yet when it comes to the how of creating such a program, the available information either skims the surface or targets only large corporations with big budgets. As a result, many small and midsized companies are dissuaded from starting giving programs and getting involved in their community because they incorrectly assume that they don't have enough money and/or resources to make a meaningful impact. My objective in writing this book was to provide you with information, tips, and examples to help you create a program that enables your company to take an active role in creating positive change in your community. Whether your company has been around for decades or you're an entrepreneur starting your business from the ground up, the examples at the end of each chapter illustrate the countless changes you can make. *All* companies have the power to make a social impact. No effort is too small.

I know that getting started can feel daunting. Be patient, stay focused, and above all, be open to change. Be prepared to change your plans, be prepared for things to not go as smoothly as you'd hoped. Not everyone will love your ideas. That's OK. Very early in my career, a manager once said to me, "The sooner you realize that you will never make everyone happy, the less stressful your life will be." I thought about those words often when we launched our program and some events didn't quite get the glowing reviews from our employees that we'd thought they would. Be open to feedback and apply it where needed. Establishing a program that's impactful, lasting, and rewarding doesn't take a million dollars, but embedding charitable activities and making "giving back" an essential part of your corporate culture takes commitment and a clear sense of mission.

Is it possible to change the world one company at a time?

Absolutely. I wish you the best of luck on your journey.

ACKNOWLEDGEMENTS

Two years ago, I decided to pursue my lifelong dream of writing a book. I have always loved books. Reading is one of my favorite hobbies, and I have often said that I could live quite comfortably in a library. Just give me a bed to sleep on and the ability to order food, and I'm good. Writing was my second love, after acting. Since an early age, I've found joy in creating characters and worlds, and reaching across the miles to connect with others via the written word. Whether it's a short story, poetry, or content for my blog, I enjoy it immensely. You could say I've always had a specific kind of book in mind for when I decided to actually pursue the dream. I thought that if I was going to take the leap into the world of publishing, it would need to be a book that would make the world a better place. I wanted to create something that would be beneficial to others.

When I started out on this journey, I knew it would be somewhat of a challenge to balance a full-time job and writing. I could not have imagined, however, just how many late nights at the laptop (way past 3 a.m. on occasion) it would entail, or the many ups and downs and twists and turns that I'd encounter along the way. Some speed bumps as well, with the occasional pothole thrown in for good measure. Working a full-time job when you don't write for a living is difficult, to say the least. I'm sure I'm not the first person to do it, and I certainly won't be the last, but it is really tough. Writing time is limited to mostly weekends and very late nights. But all that aside, I would not change a thing about this experience. I've met so many fascinating people along the way. Fellow authors, many industry experts, agents, editors, publishers. You name it. Great people with impressive backgrounds, a wealth of experience, and interesting stories that I could listen to for hours on end. I've learned a tremendous amount from them and from this process. I have cherished every moment, even the difficult ones.

I remember very clearly that day when I proudly announced to my friends and family that I was writing a book. It was a scary moment because once you put it out there, you are accountable for making it happen. Stating that I was writing a book was one of the proudest and scariest moments of my life. I remember thinking, after I hit "post" on Facebook, "There's no turning back now!"

I want to thank everyone who has provided words of encouragement, sage advice, valuable input, and candid feedback along the way. To those who listened to my ideas, listened to me whine, put up with my moods during the bumpy times, kept me on track, and held me accountable—thank you.

Thank you, Tori Eversmann, for all your guidance and advice. I had no idea what the heck I was getting into or, more to the point, where to even begin when I started out. Having someone who had been through the process and published a novel there to answer my questions (and I know they were many) was a godsend. I remember you telling me in one of our phone calls, "This process is like running a marathon when pregnant!" I thought of that phrase many times along this journey. It reassured me and kept me going whenever any doubts would creep into my head. You are fabulous, incredibly talented, and wise. I wish you continued success with your writing career and look forward to your next novel!

To Lindsey Alexander, thank you for your input, your expertise, and your amazing editing. I am indebted to you for guiding me through the complex process of book proposals and queries and everything in between. More importantly, for reviewing draft after draft of my manuscript. Your editing up front helped me immensely in this process. Thank you for keeping me on track and for preventing me from getting too far ahead of myself. I can be pretty impatient at times. You taught me that taking the time up front ensures a smoother process and high-quality product in the end. Your excitement for my project made me even more excited to share it with the world. Thanks for believing in it and for your support throughout. Your assistance has been priceless.

To Ashley Bennett, for my beautiful website. We clicked immediately (no pun intended), and you understood my vision from the get-go. From our first phone call, I knew you "got it." It was a pleasure working with you.

To Michael Weber, for allowing me to tap into that brilliant brain of yours. I am one of countless people who seek out your wisdom and advice, which you so selflessly provide. Thank you for being a sounding board on everything from illustrations and website design to the very title of this book. I will always be grateful.

To Rick Pascocello, for providing feedback on my sample chapters early on. I appreciate your time and advice. It took my manuscript to a whole other level, and I thank you.

To Brian McGinley and Daniel Winter, for your help with research and case studies. Your contributions will be so beneficial to my readers, and that is so important.

To Amy Quale, Dara Beevas, and the entire Wise Ink team, thank you for your assistance in producing this book. It has been an absolute pleasure working with you on this project. As an author, one of the most critical parts of the process is placing your project in the hands of people you can trust, and finding a publisher and team who share your values and your passion for the project. I have found all these and more in working with you. I am eternally grateful for your guidance, input, and assistance throughout this journey. I am also very proud of the way that you partner with nonprofits to support your local community.

To Alison Watts and Graham Warnken, thank you for your feedback, review, and edits. You can never have "too many eyes" on a manuscript, and I'm very thankful to have had yours.

To Nupoor Gordon for your creativity, collaboration, and beautiful artwork. Your cover art brings the message of *A Million Dollars in Change* to colorful, vibrant life. I've enjoyed working with you immensely and wish you continued success.

To Erik Gershwind, Mitchell Jacobson, and MSC Industrial Supply Co., thank you for believing in my vision and putting your faith in me to helm this important part of our company's culture. My gratitude at being given the opportunity is beyond measure and more than I could ever put into words. This book would not be possible without your support all those years ago and every day since. People tell me I have the best job. They're right.

To the many nonprofits and community groups I have worked with throughout the years, your experiences and the relationships we've forged played a big role in my decision to write this book. I thank you for the lessons you've taught me over the last decade. I hope that this book will inspire action and encourage others to become more involved in supporting their communities and nonprofit organizations. You are champions of good and catalysts of change. Never forget that. Keep pushing the for-profit world to get more involved. Together, we can truly change the world.

To my friends and family, thank you for cheering me on when it felt like I'd never reach the finish line. At times when the light at the end of the tunnel seemed more like a pinpoint, it was comforting to know that I had my cheerleaders there to lift me up and keep me on the path. To my beta readers and website testers, and all those at whom I threw sample chapters, snippets of information, and completed works for feedback—you all know who you are, and I am forever indebted to you. Thank you for taking the time out of your busy lives to indulge me and my dream by providing your observations.

Finally, to my parents, Jane and Antonio. I don't know where I'd be if not for your steadfast support and encouragement throughout this journey and throughout my life. Your example has helped shape me into the person I am today. Your selflessness, empathy, and compassion for others continue to inspire me. Thank you for being the shoulders I could lean on, particularly during a difficult time I went through on this journey, which threatened to take me off course. I am blessed and lucky to have had you there to keep me focused on what was important, and to remind me that good always triumphs in the end. Of course you were right (as always). Thanks also for dog-sitting Elvis on days when I was plowing through chapters and working on edits through the night and into the wee hours of morning. I would not have been able to do this without you.

And to Elvis, my little pup. Many a night when I was frazzled, tired, and had just about had enough, you'd come prancing over, wagging your little tail and looking for a cuddle. You always seemed to know when I needed a break, and those moments helped me to reset and jump back into my manuscript with determination. Thanks for making me a better human.

BIBLIOGRAPHY

Alexander, Alison. "The Power of Purpose: How Organizations Are Making Work More Meaningful," Northwestern University School of Education and Social Policy, 2015.

America's Charities Snapshot. "Rising Tide of Expectations: Strategies and Tools to Demonstrate Your Performance and Impact." 2014. https://www.charities.org/sites/default/files/AmChar_MemberAssembly_ Snapshot2014_051414.pdf

Aon Hewitt. "Say, Stay, or Strive? Unleash the Engagement Outcome You Need." http://www.aon.com/attachments/human-capital-consulting/2015-Drivers-of-Say-Stay-Strive.pdf

BoardSource. "Leading With Intent: A National Index of Nonprofit Board Practices." http://leadingwithintent.org/core-report/

Bridges, William. *Managing Transitions*: *Making the Most of Change.* Boston: Da Capo Lifelong Books, 2009.

Buzzfeed.com. "22 Charitable Companies That Actually Give Back." 2015.

Case Foundation. "Millennial Impact Report 2014."
www.casefoundation.org/resource/millennial-impact-report/

Charity Navigator Giving Statistics. www.charitynavigator.org

Grazer, Brian. *A Curious Mind*. New York: Simon & Schuster,
2016.

Hiatt, Jeffrey M. *ADKAR: A Model for Change in Business,
Government and Our Community*. Prosci Learning Center
Publications, 2006.

Kotter, John P. "Leading Change." Cambridge: *Harvard Business
School Press,* 1996.

Kreuser, Anne. "Boosting Employee Engagement Through
Volunteerism." Edelman. www.edelman.com/post/boosting-
employee-engagement-through-volunteerism/

Pallotta, Dan. *Charity Case: How the Nonprofit Community Can
Stand Up for Itself and Really Change the World.* Hoboken, NJ:
Jossey-Bass, 2012.

Pallotta, Dan. *Uncharitable: How Restraints on Nonprofits
Undermine Their Potential.* Tufts, 2010.

Pallotta, Dan. "The Way We Look At Charity Is Dead Wrong."
TED Talk, 2013.

Phoenix Business Journal. "Best Places to Work 2016." https://www.bizjournals.com/phoenix/news/2016/12/16/here-are-the-best-places-to-work-in-phoenix.html

"Portland Business Journal Corporate Philanthropy Award 2015." https://www.bizjournals.com/portland/event/117201/2015/corporate-philanthropy-awards-2015

Sinek, Simon. *Start With Why.* New York: Penguin/Portfolio, 2009.

Vaughn, Scott. "Mid-Sized Businesses and Social Innovation: A Revealing View." Stanford Social Innovation Review, 2013.

Welch, Jack. "How I Hire: The Must-Haves, the Definitely-Should-Haves and the Game-Changer." LinkedIn. 2013. www.linkedin.com/pulse/20130923225948-86541065-how-i-hire-the-must-haves-the-definitely-should-haves-and-the-game-changer

Welch, Jack, and Suzy Welch. *Winning: The Ultimate Business How-To Book.* New York: HarperCollins, 2005.

INDEX